100 MEDICAL MILESTONES
THAT SHAPED WORLD HISTORY

SO-1

Ruth DeJauregui

D0815915

A Bluewood book

WITHDRAWN

This edition produced and published
in 1998 by Bluewood Books
A Division of The Siyeh Group, Inc.,
P.O. Box 689
San Mateo, CA 94401

ISBN 0-912517-31-X

Printed in U.S.A.
10, 9, 8, 7, 6, 5, 4, 3, 2, 1

Designed by Stephanie Swift
Copy Edited by Greg Aaron
Edited by Colleen Turrell
Medical Editor: Alan Zacharia, M.D.

This book is not intended to provide
the reader with medical advice.
Please seek the advice of a medical
professional for any concern.

About the Author:
Ruth DeJauregui lives in
Fairfield, California, with her children.
She is a freelance writer, editor and
designer. This is her first book.

Acknowledgements: All images or
diagrams courtesy of the National
Library of Medicine with the following
exceptions; American Cancer Society:
88; American Red Cross: 89; The
Bakken Library & Museum: 61, 87;
Bayer Corporation: 54; Bluewood
Books Archive: 9, 19, 31; Eli Lily
Corporation: 80; The Eye-Bank for
Sight Restoration: 107; Integra
LifeSciences Corp: 102; The John
Hopkins School of Medicine: 25;
Alexandra Nicole Michaels: 86;
National Institute of Health: 78, 99,
105; San Mateo Imaging Center: 100;
Sandoz Pharmaceuticals: 89;
Steingrueben Archive: 29, 32, 46;
University of California San Francisco
School of Medicine: 8, 10, 11, 12,
14, 15, 16, 67, 75, 84, 91, 97, 101;
World Health Organization: 35, 69.

TABLE OF CONTENTS

1.   2. 3.   4.   5.   6. 7. 8. 9. 10.

2700 B.C.   A.D. 1   A.D. 1700

11.   12.   13.   14.   15.

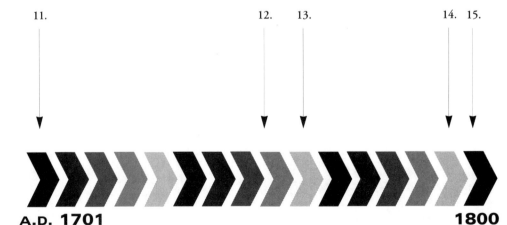

A.D. **1701**   **1800**

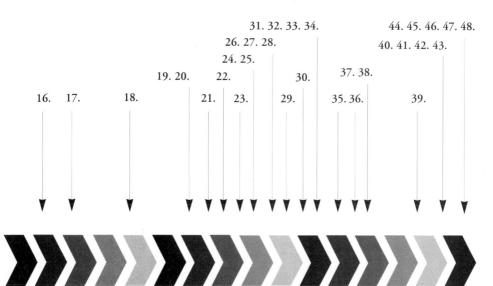

31. 32. 33. 34.   44. 45. 46. 47. 48.

26. 27. 28.   40. 41. 42. 43.

24. 25.

19. 20.   22.   30.   37. 38.

16.   17.   18.   21.   23.   29.   35. 36.   39.

1801   1900

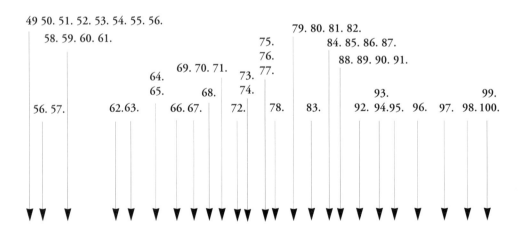

1901   2000

INTRODUCTION

The history of medicine can be thought of as a tree. First the roots began growing in many different parts of the world — China, Egypt, Greece, India and the Arab countries. As medical knowledge increased, the roots gradually came together when travelers took their knowledge back to new countries and researchers worked to find treatments for various diseases. This knowledge formed a basic understanding of the human body; the trunk of the tree. Centuries passed, and the body of medical knowledge increased dramatically. By the 20th century, the body of shared knowledge had grown so large that specialties had developed and the tree of medicine branched into the various disciplines that we know today.

The medical milestones described in this book are just 100 of the many advances that medicine has made through the centuries. Medicine has often been — and still is — a very competitive field. Many researchers have duplicated each other's findings, working independently along the same path, so there are some disputes as to who should get the credit for a particular discovery or invention. Sometimes it has been determined by who filed the first patent. Other times it was not the original discovery, but the later rediscovery, that was publicized. In many cases a new invention or technique was not considered noteworthy until it was proven to be successful or useful, sometimes many years later.

All too often, discoveries that contradicted the popular beliefs of the time were ignored. At times, researchers faced trial and possibly death for promoting new ideas. Despite many eras ruled by superstition, and in spite of social and political pressures to subscribe to certain beliefs about the body, new techniques, discoveries and inventions were developed throughout the ages. The tree of medicine just kept on growing.

Medicine is a fascinating field, with "miracle cures" and "wonder drugs." All of the drama and excitement of romance and reproduction, of life and death, lies in the history of medicine. It has shaped the lives not only of patients and doctors, but also of the peoples of the whole world. Sometimes the outcome of entire wars, such as the Crimean War, were determined not by who had the strongest army, but by whose soldiers survived the onslaught of diseases such as typhoid, typhus and cholera.

Today, many of history's great medical discoveries are taken for granted. For example, thermometers are used every day, all over the world, to check for fever. Vaccinations are a routine part of children's examinations. Habits like washing hands before handling food and brushing teeth after meals are automatic among educated people. Basic things like clean air to breathe and clean water to drink have saved millions of lives where they are widely available. And eating a balanced diet that is rich with essential vitamins is simply part of a healthy lifestyle.

Yet all of these important practices, and many others, are the result of centuries of research and development by doctors and scientists all over the world. Each new discovery is built upon the previous ones, and the next medical miracle is eagerly anticipated. Will it be acure for cancer, or for the common cold? Will it be a new gene therapy to prevent inherited diseases? Or will it be a tool to help doctors diagnose new diseases or better treat old ones?

The tree of the history of medicine continues to grow, bringing endless benefits to humankind. This book highlights just a few of the fruits of that tree. There are many other important discoveries and inventions in medical history, and you may want to explore those, too. Who knows, you might even set a new medical milestone yourself someday!

1. Herbs as Medicine
c. 2700 B.C.

The peoples of many ancient cultures all over the world used plants and herbs for healing. According to ancient Chinese legend, the emperor **Shen Nung** (or "Shennong") developed the principles of **herbal medicine** many centuries ago. The book ***Ben Cao Gang Mu (On the Use of Drugs),*** which is attributed to Shen Nung and was written around 2700 B.C., contains the first written reference to pharmacy; that is, developing drugs for medical treatments. Ancient cultures in Mesopotamia, Egypt, India, Greece and other places also left records of their uses of plants, animals and minerals for healing, although much of that ancient knowledge has been lost.

The person who made the greatest contribution to preserving such ancient knowledge was **Pedanius Dioscorides** (dye-oh-SKOR-ee-days) (fl. c. A.D. 41–68). Dioscorides was a Greek botanist who served as a surgeon in the army of the Roman Emperor. During his travels with the army, Dioscorides studied the native plants of many countries. In approximately A.D. 60, Dioscorides wrote the book *De Materia Medica (On the Use of Drugs),* which detailed the medicinal properties of more than 600 herbs as well as a number of animal products that he believed had dietetic or medicinal value.

De Materia Medica was organized according to the diseases that each plant was supposed to cure, along with a description of the plant, where it grew, how it was to be used, and an illustration. Among the plants that Dioscorides described was the juniper berry, which he said was good for coughs and stomach disorders, and the mandrake root, which he said had anesthetic qualities. Dioscorides' book was translated into almost every Western language and was used by doctors for more than 1,500 years. It is still in print.

After medical researchers began to test them, some of the traditional herbal remedies were found to be ineffective. However, many others were proven to be very helpful and were developed into important medicines. Modern doctors often use medicines derived from plants. Good examples are **aspirin** (see no. 47) and **digitalis**, used as a heart stimulant, which comes from a common garden flower. By the end of the 20th century, scientists had come to recognize the incredible pharmaceutical benefits of wild herbs and plants, and were searching the world for plants that offered new cures.

Gathering of Notable Herbalists, With Dioscorides in the Canter

Eye Surgery
750 B.C.

The study and treatment of diseases of the eye is one of the oldest fields of medicine. Around 750 B.C., the Indian surgeon **Susrata** wrote the *Susruta Samhita (Susruta's Collection),* a manual of surgery. In ancient times, doctors performed surgeries in India more than anywhere else in the world. Indian doctors had to memorize the *Susruta Samhita* before they were allowed to operate on people. Students simulated surgery by making incisions into pickles, cutting open leather bags filled with slime, and cauterizing, or searing, pieces of meat. The Inidan doctors of the time used more than 100 different steel instruments, including scalpels, probes and catheters. However, Indian doctors didn't use stitches to close wounds. Instead, they used large ants to pinch the wound closed. After the ants' pincers had gripped the flesh and closed the incision, the body of the ant was severed, leaving just the head and pincers behind, and the healing process began.

One of the procedures Susruta described was **cataract surgery**, also called "couching." Cataracts form when the clear lens of the eye gradually clouds, eventually blocking all light from entering the eye. They are caused by many different factors, but the most common factor is simply age. Even at the end of the 20th century, more than one million people went blind every year due to cataracts that formed as they got older.

Cataract surgery is fairly simple. The surgeon carefully cuts through the cornea, the transparent membrane that covers the eye, and removes it. Then the surgeon removes or displaces the clouded eye lens. Once the lens is removed from the line of vision, the person can see light again, although the eye can no longer focus properly. Eye glasses helped to correct that problem, and later, when lens transplants,

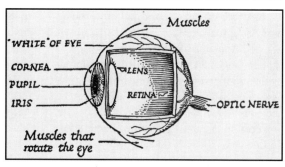

The Parts of the Eye

artificial lenses and **corneal transplants** (see no. 56) became possible, surgeons were able to restore the patient's vision.

Cataract surgery spread throughout the world and was practiced for many centuries. It was also developed independently in China during the the **Di Dynasty** (A.D. 581–618), which was a period of commercial, artistic, and scientific achievement in China. In Europe during the 16th and 17th centuries, cataract surgery was often performed by travelling "couchers" who specialized in the operation. However, as the practice of medicine grew, trained physicians eventually asserted their authority over this procedure and labelled the couchers as "quacks."

Opthalmology, the study of the eye, eventually came to study and treat many other eye problems, although cataract surgery was one of the first and most easily treated problems. **Georg Bartisch** of Konignsbruck, Germany, is seen as the founder of opthalmology. He wrote on cataracts and other eye diseases in 1583. The first detailed account of a successful cataract surgery was written by **Charles de Saint-Yves** in 1722, describing how he displaced a clouded lens into the interior of a patient's eye to restore her vision. **Jacques Daviel** in 1748 published an account of a successful lens removal and was the first to recognise that cataract is caused by a degeneration of the lens of the eye.

3. The Hippocratic Oath
c. 400 B.C.

In Greek mythology, the god of medicine was **Asclepius** (ah-SKLEE-pee-uhs), a son of the god Apollo. According to the myths, Apollo taught the art of medicine to another god, Chiron, who in turn taught it to Asclepius (who is also called "Aesculapius"). This mythological figure was probably based on a real man named Aesculapius who lived in Greece in about 1200 B.C.

An organization of craftsmen called **the Guild of Aesculapidiae** was established in the name of this god around 1250 B.C. Its members were devoted to the craft of healing. They built temples to house the sick, and in each temple was a statue of Asclepius holding a staff with a snake coiled about it. This image is called the **caduceus** (kuh-DOO-see-uss) and it has become the traditional symbol of medicine. The sick would visit these temples to pray for a cure, but they would not be admitted if they were too ill, for it was disrespectful

to the god to die in his temple. Before the sick could enter, they had to purify themselves. They could not drink wine, had to rest and diet, and were required to bathe in salt water.

Hippocrates of Cos (hi-PO-kra-teez) (460–360 B.C.) was a member of the Guild of Aesculapidiae and is internationally known as "the Father of Medicine." The code of ethics followed by the members of the guild is attributed to him and is still followed by doctors today. Essentially it states that "The doctor shall do no harm to the patient." Before beginning their practices, each doctor must swear to follow this code, which is known as taking the **Hippocratic Oath**. This is the most enduring tradition in Western medicine and has been the guiding ethical code for physicians from ancient Greece to modern times.

Although its basic tenants remain the same, the oath has been rewritten and modified over the years to adapt to changes in society. In 1948, for example, the World Medical Association issued a new oath that read in part, "The health and life of my patient will be my first consideration. ... I will not permit considerations of race, religion, nationality, party politics or social standing to intervene betwen my duty and my patient." This was in part a reaction to the horrible crimes committed by the Nazis during World War II, which included medical experiments on living people.

Hippocrates made many other important contributions to the development of medicine, including collecting facts about disease in his community, recording the symptoms of each illness, and using this information to form a basis for treatment. His careful record-keeping allowed him to judge which treatments had been most effective and prescribe them to his patients. He was the first doctor to use the principle of the **scientific method** in medicine by observing, recording, and applying his observations.

Hippocrates

4. Acupuncture
c. 100 B.C.

Chinese medicine is deeply rooted in the traditional Chinese view of the universe, began to take shape in the eighth century B.C. Chinese tradition states that there are two aspects to all processes, expressed as **yin and yang**. For example, yang is the heavens, and yin the earth; yang is hot, and yin is cold; yang is male, and yin is female. The two forces have equal power but are in constant ebb and flow, causing continual changes in the universe. In Chinese medicine, the main role of a physician has been to restore the balance of these forces. This requires the ability to control the fluctuating levels of yang and yin.

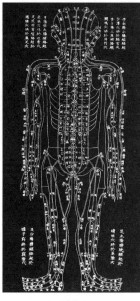

A Chinese Acupuncture Chart

Acupuncture was developed from the ancient Chinese belief that vital life energy, called **Xi** (chee), flows through the body in a series of meridians, or pathways. There are 14 meridians running through the body, circulating the yin and yang. Normally these meridians pass through deep tissues; however, there are specific points where they touch the surface. These points are where the acupuncturist inserts thin, solid needles in order to remove obstructions in the energy flow. Different meridians are related to the heart, the colon, the gallbladder, the liver, the lungs, and the other organs. Treatment with acupuncture is aimed at restoring normal energy flow so that perfect equilibrium exists throughout the body.

Acupuncture was first described in text in the book *He Yi's Cases* (c. 540 B.C.). It also appeared in the book *Shi Ji (Historical Memoirs)* by Sima Qian. However, the first definitive book on acupuncture was the *Huang di nei jing su wen, (The Book of Medicine of the Yellow Emperor)*, which dates from about 100 B.C. and also includes sections on anatomy, physiology and hygiene. Other important books are the *Muo Ching (Secrets of the Pulse)*, which explains how to diagnose diseases by feeling the patient's pulse, and the *Neijing Suwen*, which includes an instruction manual on the technique of **moxibustion**, which involves warming an acupuncture point by burning the herb mugwort over it.

While acupuncture is an ancient tradition in Chinese communities, Western medicine did not take note of it until the 1970s, when doctors in the People's Republic of China demonstrated that it could be used to control the pain induced by surgery. Some scientists believe that acupuncture helps the body to release natural pain-numbing chemicals, called endorphins, into the brain, inhibiting the transmission of pain impulses from the nerves in the body. Others think that acupuncture may work by stimulating the body to produce antibodies or cortizone, or that it may influence the autonomic nervous system, while still others feel that psychological factors are involved.

Modern medicine has learned much from traditional Chinese remedies and ideas, such as the concept of preventing disease rather than simply curing it. Preventive medicine (see no. 81) is now a part of most treatments and medical plans. By helping patients to control some of the variables in patients' lives, such as their diet, amount of excercise, and stress levels, doctors can prevent many diseases and harmful conditions from developing.

5. Dissection
c. A.D. 180

Dissection is the process of surgically taking apart a body for study. In ancient times, doctors wishing to study the body had to perform dissections very rapidly, as there was no way to preserve the body once death had occurred. They began with the internal organs, which decay more quickly; then they examined the muscles, and last they studied the bones.

The Greek doctor **Herophilus of Chalcedon** (HER-oh-FYE-luss of KAL-suh-don) (335–280 B.C.), who pioneered the practice of dissection, founded a school on anatomy, the study of the body, in Alexandria, Egypt. He based his work on knowledge of the human body gained from Egyptian embalming practices. Another Greek doctor, **Erasistratus** (uh-RA-sis-TRA-tuss) (310–250 B.C.), studied here, and the two men dissected human skulls, eyes, brains and livers. However, much of their research was lost when the great library at Alexandria was burned. No one repeated their work for centuries because human dissection was forbidden due to superstition and fear.

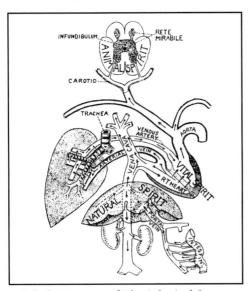

Galen's Diagram of Physiological System

The Greek doctor **Claudius Galen** (c. A.D. 129–199) revived the practice of dissection, although he never worked on humans. Other than Hippocrates (see no. 3), there is probably no other physician that has influenced the knowledge of Western medicine for a longer period of time than Galen. His medical research paved the way for important work on such things as the nervous system, the circulatory systems, and vision that would come many centuries later.

Galen practiced dissection and vivisection (dissection on a living animal) on apes, oxen and pigs. He recorded his observations about anatomy, including the functions and treatment of the many parts of the body. He also wrote down his own theories and speculations that had not been properly validated. His book, *Methodus Medendo, (Medical Knowledge by Dissection),* was written between about A.D. 180 and 190 and influenced medical practices until the 16th century.

Unfortunately, many later generations followed *Methodus Medendo* blindly, ignoring all evidence that contradicted any of Galen's beliefs. He had made some important errors, such as asserting that the chambers of the heart were perforated so that blood could pass between them. He also insisted that the heart was exactly in the center of the body, rather than slightly off to the left. Although some of Galen's ideas about human anatomy turned out to be wrong, however, his studies of muscle structures and the spinal cord were superb.

It was many centuries before others built upon Galen's work. **William of Saliceto** (c. 1210–c. 1280) published *Chirurgia (Surgery),* the earliest record of human dissection, in 1275. The Italian surgeon **Mondino de Luzzi** (c. 1275–c. 1326) supervised the first public, systematic dissection of a human body in 1315; his book *Anathomia* was the first manual of practical dissection.

As a child, Belgian physician **Andreas Vesalius** (1514–1564) was very curious about how things worked. He began to dissect small animals such as mice and frogs. As he grew older, his curiosity led him to study medicine.

By this time, human dissection was accepted in medicine. However, it was not always helpful in terms of learning the structure of the human body because surgeons at the time closely followed the teachings of **Galen** (see no. 5), which were not based on human anatamany and so were wrong in some respects. Also, the process of dissection had to be conducted rapidly — as there was no way to preserve the body and it deteriorated within a few days — so it was difficult to make new observations.

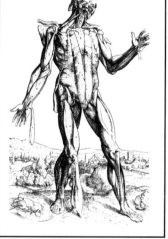

Versalius' Fifth "Muscle Man"

Vesalius was not satisfied by what he learned during these hurried dissections, so he specialized in anatomy. He became the first true authority on the subject since Galen. Although it was a crime punishable by death, he stole a corpse from the gallows in order to dissect it and learn more about the way the human body works.

After dissecting numerous bodies, Vesalius became convinced that some of Galen's ideas were wrong. Finally, when dissecting a monkey, he realized that the structures of the monkey's body closely resembled Galen's theories of anatomy. He saw that Galen's knowledge was based upon the anatomy of apes, not humans, and therefore was inaccurate.

Vesalius was not the first to discover that Galen was misled, but he was the first to publicly oppose the Catholic Church and other physicians' belief in Galen's work. The Italian artist **Leonardo da Vinci** (1452–1519) wrote the book *Anatomy* in 1510. It contained correct drawings of the human body based on cadavers that da Vinci had obtained and dissected, but he never published the book.

In 1543, Vesalius' great work was published: *De Fabrica Corporis Humani, (The Fabric of the Human Body)*. It was probably illustrated by the artist **Jan Stephen van Calcar**, who was a pupil of the Roman painter **Titian**. Each of the 300 woodcuts in the book was anatomically correct.

The book's publication set off a storm of controversy. Physicians and professors insisted that Galen's view of anatomy was the correct one, and that if anatomy was now different, then the human body must have changed. They refused to believe that the differences Vesalius found in the body's structures were due to Galen's studies of animals and wrong assumptions about human anatomy.

The Catholic Church stepped in and declared that Vesalius was wrong. Although he was the physician to the Holy Roman Emperor Charles V and his son Philip II, Vesalius was not immune to the Inquisition, a series of trials conducted by the Catholic Church as it attempted to rid the country of citizens who did not believe in its doctrines. Those who were found guilty of going against the church were sometimes tortured or killed. Vesalius was forced to make a pilgrimage to the Holy Land, which was then called Palestine, as penance. He died during his journey home.

Dressing Wounds and Stitches
1545

French surgeon **Ambroise Paré** (1510–1590) began his career as a simple barber-surgeon, trained to cut hair, shave, pull teeth, bandage wounds, and bleed patients. (At that time, doctors still believed that blood-letting — bleeding a patient through cuts or with leeches — would cure many diseases by draining harmful substances out ot the body. Sometimes they drained a pint or more of blood from a seriously ill patient. Not surprisingly, many patients did not survive this treatment.)

After a time, Paré became interested in more advanced surgery and was trained as a surgeon at the famous hospital in Paris, the **Hotel Dieu**. In those days, surgical instruments were not cleaned or sterilized after use, doctors did not wash their hands, and contagious patients were not separated from other patients. The hospital was dirty and was overrun with mice and rats. Because of these unsanitary conditions, many patients died of infection.

When he was 19 years old, Paré was recruited into the French army as the regimental surgeon, in the war against Charles V, the Holy Roman Emperor. It was during this campaign that Paré made his first medical innovation. Guns were a new tool of warfare, and gunshot wounds were deep and narrow. They became infected very easily. The usual treatment for such infection was to pour boiling oil into the wound, burning the wound closed. One day, Paré ran out of oil and was forced to improvise with a mixture of egg

Ambrose Paré

yolks, rose oil and turpentine, which he packed into the soldier's wounds. The following morning he rose early, fearful for his patients. The patients who had been treated with boiling oil were in terrible pain, with swollen wounds, from the cauterization. However, much to Paré's surprise, the patients who had been treated with the soothing lotion were resting comfortably, and they showed no signs of infection. Paré swore to never again use the boiling oil method for treating gunshot wounds because it was too cruel to the wounded men.

Despite Paré's new salve, however, many wounds still became infected. When this occured in the arms and legs, the usual treatment was amputation of the limb to prevent the infection from spreading. To stop the bleeding after an amputation, surgeons would cauterize the stump with a hot iron. Rather than use this method and cause horrible pain and scars, however, Paré developed a technique of his own: He used pieces of twine to tie the ends of bleeding veins closed.

Paré's new methods were published in his book *La Methode de Traicter les Playes (Method of Treating Wounds)* in 1545 and were quickly adopted by other surgeons in Europe, to the great relief of their patients. Paré, always modest in the face of compliments, always said about his patients who recovered successfully, "I dressed him, and God healed him."

The Circulatory System

8.

1628

The understanding of the circulation of blood in the body came gradually over many centuries. The Greek physician **Praxagoras of Cos** (c. 320–280 B.C.) was the first to discuss the arteries and veins, although he was wrong in thinking that the arteries carried air and the veins carried blood.

By the beginning of the 17th century, doctors followed **Galen's** theories on all questions of anatomy (see no. 5), many of which were wrong. For example, doctors didn't know that there was only about a gallon of blood in the body. They thought that many diseases were caused by having too much blood, and they performed blood-letting on patients with leeches in order to maintain what they thought was a proper balance.

Ideas disagreeing with Galen's views on circulation were first published in 1553 by the Spanish physician **Michael Servetus** (1511–1553). He correctly surmised that the blood passes throught the lungs in a separate step. Servetus was arrested for his views and faced the Inquisition, and later was burned at the stake.

Only six years later, the Italian anatomist **Matteo Columbo** (1516?–1559) proposed that the right and left ventricles of the heart are not perforated, as Galen had said, but are separate. He also said that the heart's right chamber pumps blood to the lungs, where it mixes with air and then returns to the left chamber to be pumped into the body. However, Columbo erroneously believe that liver to be the center of the system of veins and arteries. Like others of his time, Columbo thought that blood was manufactured in the liver, travelled to the cells, and was absorbed there in a continuous process of generation and consumption.

Andrea Cesalpino (1519–1603) was the first to propose in 1571 that the body has a circulatory system complete with tiny vessels (later called capillaries) that transfer the blood from the arteries to the veins.

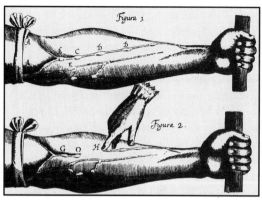

Illustration from William Harvey's Book

It wasn't until 1618 that **William Harvey** (1578–1657), a physician at the royal court and at St. Bartholomew's Hospital in London, proved that blood circulates throughout the body. Harvey's scientific experiments showed that the heart is a muscle and that its regular contractions drive the blood through the body in a coninuous process of circulation. Harvey followed Italian astronomer **Galileo Galilei's** instructions to "measure what can be measured," and he found that the heart holds two ounces of blood. His research also revealed that at 65 heartbeats per minute, the heart can pump all the blood through the body in less than one minute. Published in 1628, Harvey's 75-page book, *Exercitatio Anatomica de Mortu Cordis et Sanguinis in Animalibus (On the Movement of the Heart and Blood in Animals)*, stated his findings.

Harvey's work was not substantiated because he could not demonstrate how the blood moves from the arteries to the veins. It was the Italian doctor **Marcello Malpighi** (1628–1694) who announced in 1661 that, while using a makeshift microscope, he had observed minute capillaries connecting the arteries and veins in the lungs and intestines of frogs. His research proved Harvey correct.

9. The Microscope
1673

In 1590, the Dutch spectacle-maker **Zacharias Jansen** (1588–1631) invented the compound **microscope**. It was a significant advance over the simple single-lens magnifying glasses that were previously used, because it allowed much greater magnification of details. The anatomist **Marcello Malpighi** was the first to use a microscope in the study of anatomy, and he discovered the system of capillaries that moves blood from the veins to the arteries (see no. 8). Malpighi's work with the microscope would lead to the foundation of embryology, the study of human development within the womb.

The English chemist **Robert Hooke** (1635–1703) was the curator of experiments for the Royal Society of London, a group devoted to science. Hooke was interested in microscopes, and in 1665 he published the book *Micrographia,* which included descriptions of cells that he had seen under the microscope.

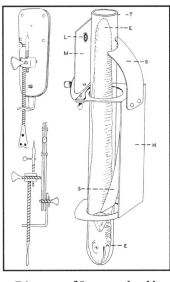

Diagram of Leeuwenhoek's Microscope

Although such observations were an interesting curiosity, however, the microscope still was not commonly used for medical research. It was not until 1673, when Dutch biologist **Anton van Leeuwenhoek** (lee-OO-wun-hoke) (1632–1723) wrote to the Royal Society that he had discovered living organisms in a drop of pond water, that the possibilities of using the microscope in medical research were realized. In another letter, he reported finding bacteria in scrapings of plaque from his own tooth. The Royal Society published his detailed pictures of such things as red blood cells and frog and eel capillaries in 1683.

Leeuwenhoek also described such tiny, one-celled organisms as bacteria, spermatozoa, and protozoans, as well as certain muscle tissues. His work laid the foundation for the theory that germs cause diseases (see no. 27).

Leeuwenhoek's pictures generated great interest, and other researchers soon began to do important work using microscopes. **Joseph Jackson Lister**, an English wine merchant and optician, improved the microscope's design and was the first to ascertain the exact form of the red blood cells. (Lister's son would go on to do work in antiseptics; see no. 31.)

The microscope has continued to be vastly important in medical research. It was essential to the discovery of the causes of such diseases as bubonic plague, malaria, yellow fever and sleeping sickness, (see nos. 40, 45 48, and 51). Once researchers were aware of the cause of a disease, they could then begin working with the virus, bacteria or parasite that caused it in order to find a vaccine or an effective medication.

The microscope is still in use in modern times to diagnose bacterial and parasitic diseases as well as cancer. It is especially important in the detection of cervical cancer through the "Pap" test, which was developed by Greek-American physician **George N. Papanicolaou** (1883–1932) in 1928. Before this test came into wide use in 1943, cervical cancer was the leading cause of death among American women; 20 years later, it had dropped to the third most common cause of death for American women.

10. Parasites
1687

The microscope (see no. 9) played an important part in the work of Italian researcher **Giovani Cosimo Bonomo** (d. 1697) and pharmacist **Diacinto Cestoni** (1637–1718), who were looking for the cause of "the itch," a contagious skin disease now known as scabies. One symptom associated with the disease is itchy, bumpy red skin that usually occurs on the hands, in elbow creases, in the armpits, in the groin area, and behind the knees.

In the 1600s, **parasites** such as lice and fleas were common, but no one had yet realized that there were even tinier creatures that infested both humans and animals. When Bonomo discovered such a creature in 1687, while looking through a microscope at a sample of skin, he realized he had found something important. He later described to a colleague what he had observed: "A minute living creature ... a little dark upon the back, with some thin, long hairs." The tiny creature that Bonomo saw, a mite called *Sarcoptes scabiei*, was the first parasite linked to a particular disease.

Bonomo noted that the creatures moved easily onto anything that came into contact with the infected skin, including towels, sheets, and clothing. He realized that the parasites would also be passed on to anyone who touched either the patient or items that had been in contact with the patient. Before this discovery, doctors could only try to relieve the symptoms of scabies with cold baths and compresses. Once they knew the cause of the disease and the method of transmission, they could at least try to prevent the spread of the parasites by disinfecting bedding and clothing by washing them in very hot water. Some doctors prescribed sulfur-based ointments to try to kill the parasites, but these were not entirely effective. Until the discovery of Lindane, a pesticide that effectively kills the microscopic mites, many patients had to just suffer through it.

Later researchers found that mites are also the source of other skin diseases such as mange, which causes the hair to fall out and scabs to form on the skin. Mites often carry bacteria, some of which can cause serious diseases like typhus (see no.58). Ticks, which are a type of large mite, also carry diseases, including Lyme disease (transmitted by the deer tick, which harbors the bacteria *Borrelia burgdorferi*) and Rocky Mountain spotted fever, (caused by the *Rickettsia* bacteria, which is carried by ticks on rodents). Modern pesticides help kill the mites, and antibiotics (see no. 70) kill the bacteria. More important, perhaps, is the concept that good personal hygiene helps to prevent diseases caused by parasites such as mites, lice and fleas.

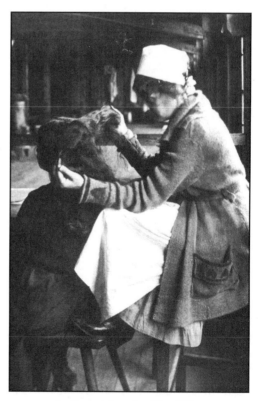

An Inspection for Head Lice

The Pulse Watch
1707

Of the many observations noted by **Galen** (see no. 5), one very important observation was the pulse, the expansion and contraction in the arteries that corresponds with the regular beating of the heart. Galen realized that measuring the rate of the pulse would give important information about the patient's health, although it was many years before anyone did further research on the pulse.

Today we know that normal pulse rate is about 60 to 70 beats per minute in adults and 80 beats per minute in children. If a patient's pulse rate is dramatically different from the normal range, there could be a significant physical problem or a heart disease such as Stokes-Adams disease, which is indicated by a slow heart beat. Heart disease that involves the pacemaker cells can result in rapid, slow, or irregular heartbeats (see no. 80).

Although doctors followed Galen's theories for hundreds of years, it wasn't until 1624 that professor **Santorio Santorius** (san-TOR-ee-

uhs) (1561–1636), at the University of Padua, Italy, invented an apparatus for measuring the pulse rate. (He also invented a crude clinical thermometer for measuring body temperature; see no. 33.) Santorius' "pulsilogium" was a simple pendulum suspended on a string; he adjusted the length of the string until the beat of the pendulum matched that of the pulse, then he measured the string.

Nearly 100 years later, in 1707, the English doctor **Sir John Floyer** (1649–1734) invented the pulse watch. Appalled that there was no standard for measuring pulse beats, Floyer took it upon himself to invent a clock to time the patient's heartbeat. His instrument was designed to run for exactly one minute and was the first clinical instrument used for medical diagnosis. He published his findings in the book *Physician's Pulse Watch*, but few people recognized the important knowledge he had contributed with this invention. However, Floyer was knighted in 1686 by James II in recognition for his other notable work as a physician, including several important books.

Today, one important use of measuring the pulse is during exercise, which is an essential part of preventive medicine (see no. 81) because proper exercise helps to prevent many diseases and unhealthful conditions. A person's target heart rate is the rate they should have during aerobic exercise like running, walking, or cycling. Aerobic exercise is the kind of exercise that specifically works the heart muscle.

To calculate your target heart rate, first subtract your age from the number 220. Then multiply this figure by a number between .70 and .95, depending on how intensely you want to work your heart — the higher the number, the more intense the workout. Divide this number by 6. Then, during your aerobic exercise, count your pulse for 10 seconds, and see if the number of heart beats matches your target heart rate. The pulse can easily be felt on the neck under the jawline, or on the wrist.

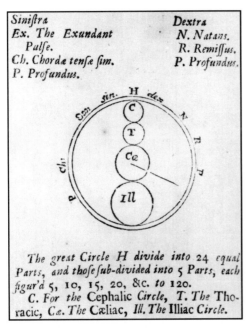

Sinistra
Ex. The Exundant Pulse.
Ch. Chordæ tensæ sim.
P. Profundus.

Dextra
N. Natans.
R. Remissus.
P. Profundus.

The great Circle H divide into 24 equal Parts, and those sub-divided into 5 Parts, each figur'd 5, 10, 15, 20, &c. to 120.
C. For the Cephalic Circle, T. The Thoracic, Cæ. The Cæliac, Ill. The Illiac Circle.

Diagram by Sir John Floyer

18

12. Scurvy
1753

Scurvy is a disease caused by a deficiency of vitamin C. It was once known as "the plague of the seas" and before the 18th century was a serious problem, especially to sailors and other travelers. The disease causes hemorrhages, bleeding of the gums, loosening of the teeth, and anemia. Anemia, lack of iron in the blood, limits the ability of the red blood cells to carry oxygen to the body's cells. For this reason, severe cases of scurvy and other diseases associated with anemia can result in death.

It has been known since ancient times that, in order to stay healthy, people need to eat a balanced diet, including protein, fats, carbohydrates, and mineral salts. However, while ships often carried animals on board to provide fresh meat, they did not typically take many fresh fruits and vegetables, because those could easily rot before the voyage was over.

In 1601, the English navigator **Sir James Lancaster** (1554–1618) wrote that lemon juice helps to prevent scurvy, but there were many other "cures" and "remedies" that were used aboard ship as well. It was not until 1753 that physician **James Lind** (1716–1794), a Scottish naval surgeon, decided to conduct experiments to determine which so-called cures were really effective. Lind experimented with 12 scurvy victims aboard the Royal Navy's *HMS. Salisbury*. He divided the men into pairs and tried each of the traditional cures for scurvy, finding that cider, nutmeg, sea water, vinegar, and a combination of garlic, mustard, and myrrh were all ineffective. However, the two scurvy patients that were given two oranges and a lemon to eat each day began to recover within six days.

Lind published his findings in 1754, and in the 1770s the famous English sea captain

Captain James Cook

James Cook (1728–1779) adopted his ideas. Cook began to give his crew citrus fruit while on long voyages. Over the next three years, while on his voyages exploring the oceans of the world, only one out of Cook's 118 sailors died of scurvy. In 1795, a British naval squadron also tested Lind's scurvy-prevention theories. It sailed for Madras, India, with rations that included lemons, and it arrived 23 weeks later with only one sailor suffering from scurvy.

From that time on, British sailors were given some lime juice to drink on every day of their voyages; thus they became known as "Limeys." The cure for scurvy had been discovered, although the essential element within citrus fruits which proved to be so important, vitamin C, was not isolated until 1928 (see no. 57).

Until 1341, it was forbidden by the Church to perform an autopsy — to cut open a human body to find out why the person had died — because the body was seen as sacred and disassembling it was thought to be disrespectful. Even after autopsy was allowed, researchers still risked excommunication or even death if the Church objected to the conclusions they drew. However, due to the work of **Andreas Vesalius** (see no. 6) and other anatomists, by the 18th century the practice of dissection to study the structure of the human body had become accepted.

The Italian physician **Giovanni Battista Morgagni** (1682–1771) published his major work, *De Sedibus et Causis Morborum per Anatomen Indagatis (On the Seats and Causes of Disease as Investigated by Anatomy)*, in 1761. His book described over 500 autopsies that compared diseased organs with healthy ones. His research, conducted over more than 40 years, introduced a concept that became the most important element in medical diagnosis: the case history. Through his autopsies, his examinations of the victims of both accidents and disease, and his case studies of patients' last illnesses, Morgagni was able to show how the outward symptoms of a disease are directly connected to changes within the body. His careful records also illustrated the importance of recording such things as a patient's life history, the progression of the disease, the events leading up to the final illness, and the manner of death.

Morgagni's work began the science of **pathological anatomy**, or the anatomy of diseased tissues. **Marie Francois Xavier Bichat** (1771–1802), a French physician, contributed to the study of pathology with his detailed identification many kinds of body tissues. Bichat named 21 different kinds of tissues in the body, and he examined the ways that diseases affect them. **Rudolf Virchow** (1821–1902), a German pathologist, later developed an important branch of pathology called cellular pathology (see no. 28).

A modern pathologist has special training in examining all the body's tissues as well as saliva, blood, urine and semen. Through careful examination, the pathologist can diagnose whether a patient died of a disease, an accident, or natural causes. A criminal pathologist can also examine a body to determine if a victim was suffocated, drowned, poisoned or otherwise murdered.

Giovanni Morgagni

14. Respiration
c. 1793

The lungs are two expandable organs located on either side of the heart and connected by a large tube, the bronchus, to the mouth. Inside the lungs are smaller tubes, the bronchioles, which lead to tiny cup-shaped air sacks called the alveoli. The alveoli are surrounded by tiny capillaries that exchange carbon dioxide from the blood stream with oxygen from the lungs in the process of respiration. During respiration, the body takes in oxygen when the person inhales, and expels carbon dioxide when the person exhales.

As blood moves throughthe circulatory system (see no. 8), it is pumped by the right ventricle of the heart to the lungs, where it recieves oxygen. Then it moves to the left ventricle, and is pumped throughout the body. This system allows the red blood cells to deliver oxygen throughout the body, and to rid the body of carbon dioxide, which is a waste product.

Until the late 18th century, respiration was a mystery. The English chemist **Robert Hooke** (1635–1703) showed that the way blood changes while in the lungs is the key feature of respiration. Hooke and English researcher **Robert Boyle** (1627–1691) showed that air is essential to life and that an animal can be kept alive by artificial respiration. But until the work of **Antoine Lavoisier** (1743–1794), what happens in the process of respiration was not understood. Lavoisier was a French chemist and physicist. He became interested in science at an early age, studying mathematics, astronomy, chemistry and botany. The discovery of the element oxygen in 1772 by Swedish chemist **Cale Wilhelm Scheele** (1742–1786) gave Lavoisier the clues that he needed to understand respiration.

In experiments on guinea pigs, Lavoisier measured how much oxygen the animals breathed in and how much water and carbon dioxide they breathed out. In his experiments using humans, the subject used a face mask to

Anton Lavoisier With His Wife

breathe oxygen while his pulse rate (see no. 11) was being counted. In this way, Lavoisier was able to measure how much oxygen was required by a person at rest. He also measured the increase in oxygen use when the subject was digesting food or doing heavy work. By 1793 he was able to show that oxygen is picked up by the tiny blood vessels in the lungs and taken to the body's cells.

Lavoisier's work on respiration helped doctors to understand the effects such conditions as asthma, which had also been studied by **John Floyer** (see no. 11). Asthma is a dangerous and sometimes fatal condition of congestion and spasms of the bronchial tubes, making breathing difficult. It is often triggered by allergies. Floyer also gave the first description of emphysema, a breathing difficulty caused by the lungs becoming enlarged with trapped air as they grow too weak to push the air out. Other respitory diseases include bronchitis, which involves acute inflammation of the bronchial tubes; and pneumonia, a deep infection of the lungs caused by bacteria that can be fatal. Respirators (see no. 65) can be helpful for people with these conditions.

15. Smallpox Vaccinations
1798

Smallpox is a contagious, often fatal disease with symptoms that include high fever and severe skin eruptions. It is caused by a **virus**, a tiny living organism that spreads either through the air or by direct contact.

Throughout history, the smallpox virus has spread from person to person in huge epidemics, with outbreaks of the disease killing thousands at a time. The first recorded description of smallpox was given by the Persian physician **Rhazes** (845–930). His simple method of identifying between such illnesses as smallpox and measles was used until the 18th century.

Between 1713 and 1716, reports on methods of smallpox inoculation were described to the **Royal Society of London**, but little attention was paid to the idea until 1718, when **Lady Mary Montagu** (1689–1762), the wife of the English minister to Constantinople, described inoculations that she had witnessed while in Turkey. A small wound was made in the arm, a few drops of **pus** from the sores of a smallpox victim was inserted into it, and a walnut shell was tied over the infected area. Although no one understood why is worked, this procedure infected patients with such a mild case of smallpox that the large majority of those treated easily recovered from the disease. Now we know that, once exposed to the virus, the body developed natural defenses to it and was able to easily fight it off if it was exposed again.

In 1721, a smallpox epidemic struck London. Lady Montagu had her five-year-old daughter inoculated in front of several leading physicians.

The result was a mild case of smallpox which immunized the child. The doctors were impressed, and **King George I** had two of his grandchildren inoculated in the same manner. The main flaw of this technique, however, was that the patients had true smallpox. They had to be completely isolated to avoid spreading the disease to others.

English physician **Edward Jenner** (1749–1823) decided in 1796 to test the theory that contracting a case of cowpox provided immunity to smallpox. Cowpox is a disease that affects cows very much the way smallpox affects people, and it can be contracted by humans in a mild form. Jenner took some of the fluid from cowpox sores on the hands of a dairymaid, and scratched it into the skin of an eight-year-old schoolboy, **James Phipps**. A few weeks later he inoculated the boy with smallpox. Unlike the other children who had been inoculated with it, Phipps did not contract smallpox. Jenner continued his experiments for two more years before publishing his results, *Inquiry into the Cause and Effects of the Variolae Vaccinae,* in 1798. His experiments laid the foundation of immunology, the study of the body's responses to foreign substances (see no. 44).

In 1799, the first U.S. vaccinations against smallpox were given by Harvard medical professor **Benjamin Waterhouse** (1754–1846) to his five-year-old son. Vaccination programs against smallpox were promoted vigorously around the world over the next 180 years, and by the end of the 1970s, the disease had been completely eliminated.

Dairymaid's Hand Infected with Cowpox

The **nervous system** is made up of the brain, the spinal cord and the nerves. The nerve cells collect information from the environment through the five senses — sight, touch, taste, smell and hearing — and carry the information through the spinal cord to the brain, which interprets it. The brain also stores memories and creates adaptive behaviors.

The Greek physicians **Herophilus** and **Erasistratus** studied the human brain as part of their dissections (see no. 5), and **Galen** studied the brain and the nerves in animals (see no. 5). However, the nervous system was poorly understood until 1664, when English physician **Thomas Willis** (1621– 1675) published the most comprehensive and accurate description of the nervous systemup to that time in his book *Cerebri Anatome (Anatomy of the Brain).*

Other researchers continued to study the central nervous system. Scottish physician **Robert Whytt** (1714–1766) in 1751 made a distinction between voluntary and involuntary motion. This demonstrated that some movements of the body, such as reflex movements, happen without a person consciously willing them. In 1809, **Luigi Rolando** of Sardinia (1773–1831) described his observations of experiments on animals showing that the two hemispheres of the brain affect different sides of the body.

Meanwhile, **Sir Charles Bell** (1774–1842) was interested in why and how the human body works. He was fascinated by the way that nerves function. Through much experimentation on laboratory animals, cutting certain nerves and recording the functions that were lost, Bell demonstrated that certain nerves, the "motor reflex nerves," transmit impulses for movement from the brain to the muscles of the body, while other nerves, the "sensory nerves," transmit sensations from the body to the brain. Bell published his findings in 1811 in his book *Idea of a New Anatomy of the*

Sir Charles Bell

Brain. This book formed the basis of the modern understanding of the brain. The nerve actions he discovered is now known as the "Bell-Magendie law" in reference to the French physiologist **Francois Magendie** (1783–1855), who showed that the motor nerves stem form the anterior root of the spinal canal and the sensory nerves stem form the posterior root.

Nearly 50 years later, English researcher **Sir Charles Scott Sherrington** (1857–1952) took up the study of the nervous system. He conducted a long series of animal experiments. By removing different sections of the brain and studying the reflexes of the disabled animal, he discovered how the remaining spinal nerves acted together. He found that when one set of muscles was stimulated, an opposing set was inhibited. By determining the connections in the brain stem and the spinal cord, Sherrington established the interrelationships of the muscular and nervous systems, and he discovered how reflexes affect movement. His book *The Integrative Action of the Nervous System* was published in 1906.

17. The Stethoscope
1816

French doctor **René Théophile Hyacinthe Laënnec** (1781–1826) was a modest individual. When in 1816 a young woman patient complained of chest pain, he was too embarrassed to put his ear to her chest. Despite the fact that doctors from the time of ancient Greece had used this method to listen to the heartbeat, he simply could not do it. Uncertain as to how to proceed, he remembered observing children playing with a hollow log, one child tapping on one end, and the second child listening at the other. He then took some paper, rolled it into the shape of a tube, and placed one end against the woman's chest and the other end against his ear. To his surprise, not only could he

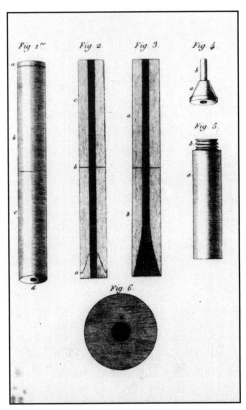

Laënnec's Stethoscope

hear her heartbeat, but the sound was clearer than he had ever heard before! Laënnec immediately set about developing a tool like the hollow tube that he could use with all his patients.

Laënnec's first real **stethoscope** was a wooden tube that he made himself. It was nine inches (23 cm) long and 1.5 inches (4 cm) wide. With this new device, he observed and recorded the symptoms of his patient's illnesses and noted the sounds made in their chests. After he had compiled a number of case studies, Laënnec was able to link certain abnormal chest sounds to specific diseases. This was the first time that an artificial device or machine had been used to diagnose heart and lung diseases. With this new invention, Laënnec advanced the practice of **auscultation** (ah-skul-TAY-shen), or monitoring the sounds made by the internal organs.

Laënnec's wooden stethoscopes were used until 1850. Awkward and difficult to use, they were eventually replaced by rubber tubing, and in 1852, the American doctor **George Cammann** added earpieces. After microphones were invented in 1878 by **D.E. Hughes**, a microphone was added to the chest piece of the stethoscope to magnify the sound even further.

Laënnec's particular interest, for which the use of the stethoscope became essential, was the study of tuberculosis (see no. 39), a common and sometimes fatal disease that typically affects the lungs. By listening with the stethoscope as the patient breathed, he could detect the accumulated fluid in the lungs. Laënnec found that more than half of the patients that came to the hospital had tuberculosis. He conducted more than a thousand autopsies, showing that the disease could appear in any part of the body as small lumps called "tubercles." Tragically, Laënnec died in 1826 of the very disease he had spent so much time studying.

24

18. Blood Transfusions
1829

Research into **blood transfusions** was made possible by the work of English architect and natural philosopher **Sir Christopher Wren** (1632–1723). In 1657, he performed a series of experiments on animals, injecting various fluids into their veins to cause vomiting, purging, intoxication and other conditions. The **Royal Society of London** became interested in the role of blood in the body, and in 1665 **John Wilkins** (1614–1672), a member of the Royal Society, drew blood from a dog and then injected it into another dog.

The first direct transfusion of blood from one animal to another was performed in 1666 by English researcher and Royal Society member **Richard Lower** (1631–1691). He first used a hollow quill to connect the animals' blood vessels, but he later began using silver tubes. Since blood was believed to be the ingredient that passed on hereditary traits (see nos. 32, 53 and 75), there was much speculation as to the results of a transfusion. By drawing the blood out of one animal and putting it into another, the researchers asked, would the recipient become more like the donor? If a sheep was transfused with the blood of a dog, would it begin to bark? Of course, it didn't. What did happen was that sometimes the animal lived and sometimes it died.

The first human transfusion occurred in 1667 when a French physician, **Jean-Baptiste Denis** (1625–1704), doctor to **King Louis IV**, transfused the blood of a lamb into a 15-year-old boy. Fortunately the boy survived, but transfusions proved to be so dangerous

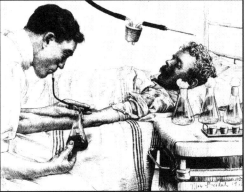

A Blood Transfusion

that physicians soon ceased to conduct them. Although doctors knew that blood transfusions could help to keep their patient's alive, few blood transfusions were attempted again until the 19th century.

English physician and obstetrician **James Blundell** (1790–1878) thought he could do a transfusion safely if the dondor blood came from the same species. While he was professor of physiology and obstetrics at Guy's Hospital from 1823 to 1834, he began using a syringe (see no. 24) to transfuse blood from his assistants to dying patients. In 1829, one of his patients, a young woman who was bleeding heavily after giving birth, received a transfusion and survived. Encouraged, Blundell continued with his experiments, but problems soon arose. Sometimes the new blood was fine, but other times it would clump together after being transfused into the patient, causing jaundice (yellowing of the skin and eyes), kidney damage, and sometimes death. Blundell did not understand why this would happen. It was not until 1902 that **Karl Landsteiner** found the answer when he identified the four different blood types (see no. 50).

After many years of research, blood transfusions eventually became safe for patients. Blood banks were widely established, and volunteers donated blood to them on a regular basis. Blood transfusions have now become an essential part of medicine. In the late 1990s, an average of more than two million blood transfusions were performed in the United States every year.

Public Health
1842

During the early 1800s, because of the Industrial Revolution, there was a demand for many workers. People in Europe and America began to move from the countryside into the industrial cities, meeting the demand for work in the new factories. However, their overcrowded living conditions in the cities led to unsanitary living quarters. In London, England, for example, sewage disposal became a big problem. The stench of raw sewage in the River Thames was so bad that Parliament assigned **Sir Edwin Chadwick** (1800–1890), a lawyer and journalist, to investigate the causes.

Chadwick's report, *Sanitary Conditions of the Labouring Population of Great Britain,* came out in 1842. He found that poor people were more likely to catch infectious diseases and that they and their children died more often than children of the affluent. He attributed this to their poor living conditions. Families were crowded into tiny flats or apartments, allowing diseases to spread easily from person to person because there was no way to

Sir Edwin Chadwick

isolate the sick. Caregivers did not wash their hands after caring for patients and before preparing food. Rats and other pests ran unchecked through the homes of the poor, and there was no way to properly store fresh foods to keep them free of molds and bugs.

According to Chadwick's report, only one in eight of England's towns had clean drinking water. He stated that trash should be removed from the streets and that the water should be cleaned by removing the raw waste from the sewer drains which poured directly into the Thames. Although Chadwick was right, Parliament was unable to agree to it and did not pass laws strong enough to have any effect. As time went on, new discoveries would prove Chadwick correct (see nos. 21 and 81).

By the next century, Chadwick's proposals became more and more popular. The public became aware of the importance of clean water, air and food. One early sign of environmental degradation was the air pollution caused by the growing factories. As technology progressed, pollution problems rose in all industrialized areas as well as in rivers, lakes and the ocean. Pesticides poisoned fish and wildlife, and industrial-waste products contaminated drinking water. By the end of the 20th century, many diseases and cancers had been linked to environmental factors such as contaminated air and water. The treatment of drinking water with chlorine, which was first introduced in 1800, protects the public from many dangerous organisms like the protozoa *Giardia lamblia* and the bacteria *E. coli,* as well as the bacteria that cause cholera (see no. 25), typhoid (see no. 46), and other diseases.

Public health offices now exist in nearly every country of the world to promote such things as cleanliness, pest control, and vaccination programs. Because of these measures, many epidemic diseases, including smallpox, polio and measles, have been nearly eliminated.

Before **anesthetics** came into widespread use, most patients had to endure surgical procedures without any relief from pain. A kind of anesthetic was first used by the Dominican monk **Friar Theodoric of Lucca** as early as 1236. He induced sleep in his patients by having them drink a liquid containing a form of the drug opium, or by soaking a sponge in the liquid and putting it over the patient's nose. However, this practice was extremely rare.

In 1795, the English chemist **Sir Humphrey Davy** (1778–1829) discovered nitrous oxide, also known as laughing gas. After inhaling the gas, he found that he was both intoxicated and immune to pain. He thought that the gas might be useful in medicine as an anesthetic, and he published his findings in 1800. However, nitrous oxide was generally used as a novelty shown for amusement in public exhibitions until 1843,

William T.G. Morton

when dentist **Horace Wells** (1819–1868) learned about laughing gas after watching a demonstration by a showman. Wells had his own tooth extracted after inhaling the gas, and finding that it worked, he painlessly extracted the teeth of 15 patients while using the gas. On December 11, 1844, Wells demonstrated the gas at **Harvard Medical School**, but when he pulled the patient's tooth, the young boy cried out. The class was not impressed, and derided Wells for his attempt.

In the meantime, experiments were taking place on another anesthetic substance, sulfuric ether. A chemistry student by the name of **William Clarke** used ether on a woman whose tooth was extracted in January 1842. In the first verified use of general anesthetic during surgery, American surgeon **Crawford Long** (1815–1878) removed a cyst from a man's neck on March 30, 1842, while the patient inhaled ether. Two years later, Long administered ether to his wife while she gave birth to their child. However, Long did not publish his work on anesthetics for another seven years.

Another Boston dentist, **William Thomas Green Morton** (1819–1868), heard a lecture on sulfuric ether by the chemist Charles T. Jackson. Morton was not familiar with ether's anesthetic properties and was surprised to find that it could cause a person to become unconscious. He experimented on himself and his dog, and later used it when pulling a patient's tooth. Morton was persuaded to give a public demonstration of his methods at **Massachusetts General Hospital**. On October 16, 1846, Morton used ether during an operation to remove a tumor from a patient's jaw. Newspapers ran the story the next day, and doctors soon began to use ether more frequently.

The use of ether, spread rapidly, in part because of the outbreak of the **Mexican War** in 1846. During the war, it was used on the casualties to relieve their pain during surgery. However, the greatest breakthrough in public acceptance of anesthetic came when **Queen Victoria** (1819–1901) used it during childbirth. After that, anesthetics were used frequently in surgery and dentistry, beginning a new age in medicine.

21. The Science of Epidemiology
1846

One of the first doctors to study **epidemics**, English physician **Thomas Sydenham** (1624– 1689) made clear distinctions between different diseases and provided the classic descriptions of cholera, gout, malaria, scarlet fever and smallpox. He proposed that researchers should observe, rather than theorize, to discover the characteristics of diseases.

Sydenham's work laid the framework for Danish physician **Peter Panum's** (1820–1885) research in the Faroe Islands, in the north Atlantic, in 1846. In modern times, measles (a disease characterized by fever, weakness, sore muscles, headache, eye irritation, sensitivity to light and skin rash) is easily prevented by vaccination. However, in the 19th century, measles was an epidemic disease, spreading rapidly and killing thousands of people. Panum was asked by the Danish government to go to the Faroe Islands to study the disease. By studying the history of measles epidemics among the Faroe Islanders, Panum recognized that the isolated groups of islanders did not have any resistance to imported diseases. Therefore, when the people were exposed to a new virus, they were devastated. In 1876, this theory was confirmed when a British cruiser arrived in Fiji with a sailor suffering from measles. Lacking any natural resistance to the disease, a quarter of Fiji's population died within three months.

Panum's research began the formal science of epidemiology. In 1854, English physician **John Simon** (1816–1904) was appointed London's first medical officer of health. He created a public health service that became a

Thomas Sydenham

model for other nations. Building on the theories of **Edwin Chadwick** (see no. 19) and Panum, Simon investigated the spread of diseases in London, particularly in the slums. He showed how environmental conditions can influence the severity of an epidemic.

Today, epidemiologists use field investigations, laboratory techniques, statistical analysis and computers to investigate how and where a disease begins, how it spreads, who it affects, and how to control and prevent it. Early epidemiologists concentrated on tuberculosis (see no. 39), influenza (also called "the flu") and cholera (see no. 25), but now they also investigate such diseases as cancer (see no. 34), heart disease, and AIDS (see no. 96) which affect large groups of people. In addition to the work of epidemiologists, vaccinations (see no. 15) have also helped to slow the spread of many diseases, including measles. The measles vaccine became available in 1963, and in the following three years the number of cases in the U.S. fell from 482,000 to just 22,000.

Epidemiology today studies how widescale changes in medical practices, diet and lifestyle can affect disease rates in large groups of people. For example, heart disease, which can be brought about by such lifestyle factors as smoking, obesity and lack of exercise, reached epidemic proportions in the U.S. during the 1960s. Educational programs promoting a healthier lifestyle have helped many people avoid heart disease, and rates are declining.

22. Preventing Infection
1847

In 1843, Boston writer and physician **Oliver Wendell Holmes, Sr.** (1809–1894) published an outraged commentary on the contagiousness of childbed (puerperal) fever. We now know that this disease is caused by bacteria on the unwashed hands of a midwife or doctor that infects the mother's uterus during childbirth. It is usually caused by the bacteria *Streptococcus pyogenes* (strep-tuh-KOK-suss pye-OH-juh-neez). However, in Holmes' time, the cause of the disease was a mystery.

Holmes studied reports on various hospitals and their death rates, and he concluded that the cleaner the maternity ward was, the lower the death rate of new mothers would be. He blamed doctors for the spread of the disease and urged them to wash their hands and wear clean clothes in the maternity wards.

Holmes' research was followed in 1847 by that of the Hungarian obstetrician **Ignaz Philipp Semmelweis** (1818–1865), who proved that childbed fever is contagious. Semmelweis found that by rigidly enforcing personal hygiene among the examining students in the hospital, new mothers would not be infected with childbed fever. He insisted that physicians wash their hands in chlorinated water. This practice reduced the death rate from 9.92 percent to 1.27 percent in just two years. Semmelweis returned to Hungary in 1850 and began to enforce his practices at St. Rochus Hospital.

Although Semmelweis' ideas about infection faced opposition from the Viennese hospital authorities, he still rose to become professor of obstetrics at the University of Budapest in 1854. He did not gain the recognition he deserved, however, until after his death, when English surgeon **Joseph Lister** (1827– 1912) proved his ideas through the use of germ-killing antiseptics (see no. 31). Sadly, Semmelweis died from the same bacteria that causes childbed fever. *Streptococcus pyogenes* invaded a cut in his hand and caused a high fever as it spread through the blood. He died of septicema, or blood poisoning, when the infection spread throughout his body.

After Semmelweis' work was accepted in the medical profession, many doctors, including the surgeon-in-chief and professor of surgery at Johns Hopkins Medical School, the American doctor **William Stewart Halsted** (1852–1922), made their medical staff scrub with a solution of mercuric chloride. One of Halsted's nurses complained of skin irritation from the harsh chemicals, so Halsted asked the Goodyear Rubber Company to make her some thin rubber gloves. They were so effective that Halsted soon ordered gloves for his entire staff. The practice of wearing gloves during surgery spread rapidly.

In modern times, rubber gloves are an important part of disease control, especially since the advent of AIDS (see no. 96). Not only doctors and nurses, but also dentists, emergency medical technicians, police officers and many others now wear gloves to prevent contact with contagious substances.

Ignaz Semmelweis

23. The Ophthalmoscope
1851

Hermann Ludwig Ferdinand von Helmholtz (1821–1894) was a German scientist and optics researcher who also investigated electrodynamics (the study of the electromagnetic force of electrons), mathematics and meteorology. He and several associates formed the "mechanistic school" of physiology, which attempted to explain the workings of the body in terms of physics and chemistry. Between 1843 and 1847, Helmholtz published a series of papers in which he applied these principles to demonstrate how the body burns energy and how nerve impulses travel through the body at a measurable speed.

In 1851, Helmholtz invented the **ophthalmoscope** (op-THAL-muh-scope), an instrument used to view the inside of the eye. He wanted to examine the structures of the eye and look for diseases in it.

The first ophthalmoscope consisted of a mirror with a hole in the center and a set of magnifying lenses. Two parallel beams of light were shined into the eye, and the doctor was able to look through the device to observe the interior of the eye. Helmholtz also invented the **opthalmometer**, a device that measures the curvature of the eye, and he did important work on the theory that vision functions using the three primary colors.

Before the invention of the ophthalmoscope, doctors had used a simple magnifying glass to look at the eye. With the new instrument, doctors could easily examine the retina (the light-sensitive part at the back of the eye), the blood vessels at the back of the eye, and the optic nerve. Later ophthalmoscopes were modified by the Swedish doctor **Allvar Gullstrand**, who improved the instrument enough to enlarge images between five and 40 times. Modern ophthalmologists, doctors who specialize in the treatment of eye diseases, examine the inside of the eye with an ophthalmoscope to diagnose problems like glaucoma, which is caused by diabetes; cataract, opacity of the lens of the eye; trachoma, an infectious disease caused by the *Chlamydia* bacteria, and injuries to the eye from foreign matter and sharp objects. They can also check for evidence of chronic high blood pressure and examine tumors of the inner eye.

In addition to diagnosis, a surgeon can perform surgery on the eye using a modern ophthalmoscope. Further developments have included the addition of the laser (see no. 84). By using a laser beam, a surgeon can weld a detached retina into place on the back of the eye or can remove tumors. Lasers can also be used to measure a patient's blood circulation. The doctor aims a low-level laser beam on a vein at the back of the eye and measures the speed of the reflected light to determine the rate of circulation.

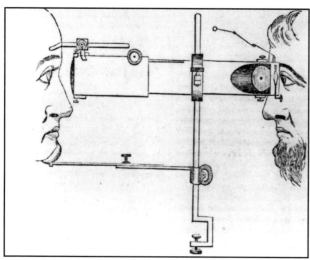

A Doctor Using an Opthalmoscope

The syringe is an instrument that consists of a hollow barrell fitted with a plunger on one end and an opening on the other. The barrel is filled with liquid, and the plunger is pressed, forcing the liquid out through the hole. Until the invention of the **hypodermic syringe**, a syringe with a needle tip that can inject liquid under the skin, doctors used simple syringes that were just a hollow tube. These first syringes could only be used in natural openings of the body or if the doctor cut through the skin first.

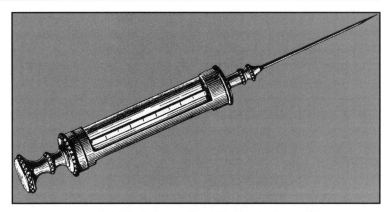

A 19th-Century Hypodermic Syringe

Syringes have been used as early as the time of **Galen** (see no. 5). When **William Harvey** (see no. 8) studied circulation hundreds of years later, he used a hollow-tube syringe with a point at one end to inject dye into an animal's vein to study where the blood moved in its body.

In 1713, French surgeon **Dominique Anel** (1679–1730) invented a fine-point syringe, which he used in operating on a tear duct in his patient's eye. In 1853, French orthopedic surgeon **Charles Gabriel Pravaz** (1791–1853) took this idea a step further and added a thin hollow needle to the syringe, creating the hypodermic syringe and at last enabling doctors to inject directly under the skin. ("Hypo" is a Greek word that means "under"; "dermic" is derived from the Greek word for "skin".) Two years later, the Scottish doctor **Alexander Wood** (1817–1864) injected a patient with morphine, an anesthetic, for the first time.

With the introduction of the hypodermic syringe, doctors were able to inject not only painkillers, but also vaccines and other substances. If injected directly under the skin, medications like the smallpox vaccine could be quickly and almost painlessly administered. Furthermore, medications that are injected into the bloodstream are absorbed by the body at a faster rate than those which are taken orally. Some anesthetics are normally injected at the place where they can be most effective. These include spinal anesthetics, used primarily for lower body surgery, epidural anesthetics for childbirth, and other local anesthetics like Novocain and lidocaine, which are frequently used during dental procedures.

There have been a number of improvements to the hypodermic syringe. Needles have been developed that are completely disposable, avoiding the need to sterilize them for reuse. In 1997, a needle "guard" was developed to protect medical staff from accidental needle sticks, which are now a serious concern because of the AIDS epidemic (see no. 96). Once the injection is complete, the needle is no longer exposed, and can be disposed of without fear of accidental exposure to HIV, hepatitis or other dangerous diseases that are spread through contact with infected blood.

Through the centuries, epidemics of **cholera** have occurred in nearly every part of the world. The bacteria that causes this disease is found in food and water contaminated by sewage, and in raw or undercooked seafood. The disease spreads quickly, causing sudden diarrhea and vomiting, muscle cramps, and severe dehydration that can prove fatal

During an epidemic of cholera in London in 1853, physician **John Snow** (1813–1858), who had introduced ether into British surgery in 1847, traced the disease to a public pump on Broad Street. He located the area where the epidemic was centered and found that every family affected had used that particular pump for their water. He had already suggested that since cholera was centered in the digestive system, it must be transmitted through something that is ingested. When officials asked how to stop the epidemic,

John Snow

Snow told them to remove the handle of the busy public pump. The following year, after months of research was complete, it was proved that the water supply for that pump was contaminated by the cesspool of a building where a cholera patient lived.

Like many previous medical discoveries, Snow's theory was virtually ignored for many years, even though it had been clearly demonstrated. It was not until 1881 that Spanish bacteriologist **Jaime Ferrán y Clua** (1852–1929) developed a serum that could prevent cholera. However, it contained active cholera bacteria. After testing it on himself, he allowed his new vaccine to be given to 50,000 people. Tragically, some of the people who received his vaccine died of the disease.

In 1884, German researcher **Robert Koch** (1843–1910) (see nos. 37and 38) discovered the bacteria *Vibrio cholerae,* which is responsible for cholera. Koch had been appointed as the leader of a German expedition sent to Egypt and India to investigate cholera epidemics. His careful work and previous experience in isolating the bacterias that cause anthrax, tuberculosis and conjunctivitis (a disease in which the mucous membrane of the eye becomes inflamed) helped him succeed in finding the cholera bacteria. For his work, Koch was awarded a Nobel Prize in 1905.

In spite of all the advances in our understanding of how diseases are spread, many people in the world still live in overcrowded, unsanitary conditions. Cholera still exists and is still fatal, despite the fact that there are effective antibiotics, a vaccine, and many helpful treatments. One important treatment for cholera victims is an intravenous saline solution or an inexpensive drink of an electrolyte solution made of water, sugar, salt and baking soda. These fluids helps victims of cholera survive the severe dehydration associated with the disease.

Digestion
1857

Digestion is the process by which food — proteins, fats and carbohydrates — is chemically broken down into sugar that the body's cells can absorb. In several stages, digestive enzymes break down food into amino acids, fatty acids, glycerol, and sugar, which is absorbed, along with vitamins and minerals, through the intestines and into the bloodstream.

William Beaumont (1785–1853) was the first to study the digestive system in action. An American doctor, he did not attend a medical school but was apprenticed to a practicing doctor, and after two years he enlisted in the army as an assistant surgeon during the War of 1812. After the war, Beaumont was stationed at the trading post and fort at Mackinac, Michigan. There he operated on **Alexis Saint Martin**, who had been shot in the stomach, in 1822. When he was brought to Beaumont, Saint Martin was expected to die. Saint Martin survived, but he was left with a permanent hole in his stomach, which allowed Beaumont to study the digestive process.

Beaumont took full advantage of this opportunity. He observed the digestive fluids breaking down food and watched how the muscles in the stomach then pushed the food into the small intestines for further absorption into the body. He carefully recorded the time and amount of food eaten and how long it took for the stomach to work. Beaumont's discoveries revolutionized ideas about the stomach and how it functions. His experiments were published in 1833 in his book, *Experiments and Observations on the Gastric Juice and the Physiology of Digestion*.

The same year that Beaumont published his findings, a French researcher discovered a catalyst in malt that helps to ferment beer. He called this catalyst "diatase." It was only two years later, in 1835, that German anatomist **Theodor Schwann** (1810–1882) found that a similar substance is produced in the body. He extracted a substance from the stomach that he

Claude Bernard

called "pepsin," and announced that this was an essential ingredient of the digestive fluids.

The French doctor **Claude Bernard** (1813–1878) expanded upon Beaumont and Schwann's discoveries. Bernard used animals in his work, recording what he had fed them and how long the food took to digest and to affect the body through the bloodstream. In 1857, Bernard isolated glycogen, a large molecule in the blood that changes to sugar in the liver. He also showed that the pancreas plays a role in the digestion of fats.

It wasn't until 1883 that German researcher **Wilhelm Kuhne** (1837–1900) coined the word "enzymes" to describe the active molecules in the digestive fluids. Kuhne showed how both digestion and beer brewing utilize enzymes, and how they break down food into its components. Without enzymes, the temperature of the human body would have to rise to 572° F to digest food!

In the 17th century, doctors believed that maggots grew spontaneously from rotting meat in an example of what was called "spontaneous generation." In 1668, Italian physician and naturalist **Francesco Redi** (1627–1697) tested this theory by placing meat in jars to attract flies. Some of the jars were covered with gauze, and others were left open. Flies were soon attracted to the rotting meat. However, the meat in the covered jars never developed maggots, although maggots did appear on top of the gauze, while the meat in all of the uncovered jars was infested. Redi thus proved that flies, not something in the rotting meat, produced the maggots.

It was nearly 200 years before French researcher **Louis Pasteur** (1822–1895) followed in Redi's footsteps and attempted to demonstrate that bacteria are produced by other bacteria, not by some mysterious process. Pasteur was a chemist, yet today his work influences everything from vaccinations to the milk sold at the grocery store. In 1857, Pasteur demonstrated that fermentation, the breakdown of organic compounds, can be caused by bacteria.

He showed this by boiling a nutrient solution to sterilize it, then filtering the air entering the flask holding the solution so that no bacteria could enter it from the outside. Upon repeated checks Pasteur found that no bacteria appeared in his solution, and thus he again disproved the spontaneous generation theory.

Pasteur found that by destroying the bacteria and preventing further contamination, he could stop the fermentation process. Among the microorganisms he had destroyed were the ones that cause grape juice to ferment and change into wine. More important was the fact that Pasteur realized that he had also found the cause of many diseases in the bacteria ("germs") that are transmitted to people through contaminated food or beverages. This idea became known as **the germ theory of disease**.

Later, Pasteur experimented with disinfecting various foods and found that heating milk to exactly 135° F (57.2° C) kills the harmful bacteria. This discovery revolutionized medicine. Doctors would eventually identify the different bacteria responsible for different diseases and would take measures to kill the bacteria to prevent infections from starting (see no. 31, antiseptics). Meanwhile, Pasteur developed the process of pasteurization (pass-tyer-i-ZAY-shen), the treatment of food with heat to destroy the bacteria that cause diseases such as typhoid (see no. 46) and tuberculosis (see no. 39).

In 1868 Pasteur suffered a stroke and was paralyzed for a time. After he recovered from his illness, he continued his research on bacteria and diseases and developed many important vaccinations (see no. 38).

Louis Pasteur

The word "cell" was coined in 1665 by the English chemist **Robert Hooke** (see no. 14), who described cells as the "many little boxes" he saw while examining corkwood under a microscope (see no. 9). The German physiologist **Theodor Schwann** (1810–1882) discovered that animals as well as plants are comprised of cells, but he didn't know where the cells came from and thought they arose spontaneously out of thin air. It was not until 1858, when Prussian pathologist **Rudolf Virchow** (1821–1902) analyzed the cell formation and structure of diseased tissues that it became clear that, rather than forming spontaneously, all cells derive from other cells.

Virchow used the microscope to look at how diseased cells change. He watched one cell divide into two equal parts and noticed that, as the cells multiplied, the diseased tissues multiplied, too.

With these discoveries, Virchow set the groundwork for the "cell theory of life." He showed that all body tissues and organs are made of cells, that all cells are produced from other cells, that many diseases are the result of changes in cells, and that one could identify some diseases by the appearance of the cells. Later researchers refined the theory to six basic ideas: cells are the basic unit of life; all living things are comprised of cells; all cells are descended from previous cells, through either division ("mitosis") or the combination of two sex cells; cells are surrounded by a membrane that separates them from each other; and all cells are small (most are not detectable to the naked human eye).

It was later understood that, although most cells divide for a time and then die, cancer cells continue to reproduce rapidly, forming into dense, harmful tumors that crowd out the normal tissues (see no. 34). Along with describing cell division, Virchow identified leukemia (cancer of the blood) and

Rudolf Virchow

thrombosis (the clogging of blood vessels with blood clots).

Virchow is now known as the founder of cellular pathology, which is the study of disease by examining the cells of tissues and bodily fluids obtained during surgery or autopsy. He established the Pathological Institute and Museum in Berlin, which at the time of his death contained more than 23,000 specimens of body tissues and organs. His books include *Cellular Pathology as Based on History* (1850), *Famine Fever* (1868), *Freedom of Science* (1878) and *Post-mortem Examinations* (1878).

Virchow also called for many reforms to improve public health (see no. 19), such as better public sewage systems and cleaner hospitals and schools, as well as the proper inspection of meat and other easily contaminated foods.

Measuring Blood Pressure
1860

Measuring the pressure of blood flow in the circulatory system (see no. 8) can be done through applying an equal amont of pressure on the outside of the body, and measuring that. However, there are two different pressure readings: systolic pressure, which is the pressure of the blood on the pulse beat, and diastolic pressure, which measures the blood pressure between pulses.

When researchers first tried to measure blood pressure in animals, they cut into an artery and inserted a narrow column of glass that was marked in millimeters and was partially filled with mercury, which bobbed up and down in time to the heart's beating. English researcher **Stephen Hales** published his findings based on this method in 1733. In 1881, **Samuel Siegfried von Bash** described his ideas for a similar instrument that did not require breaking the skin.

Jules Hérisson constructed such an instrument, now called the **sphygmomanometer** (sfig-moh-muh-NOM-ee-ter), in 1835.

Although this instrument was difficult to use, it allowed doctors to concurrently measure both the pulse and the blood pressure for the first time. Not satisfied with Herisson's awkward instrument, French physiologist **Etienne Jules Marey** (1830–1904) in 1860 designed a better way to measure blood pressure. His **sphygmomanograph** magnified the movement of the pulse, transferring the beat onto paper. Besides making a permanent record, Marey's invention could be carried from patient to patient. He used it to study what causes irregular heartbeats. Soon, doctors began to accumulate a body of evidence on blood pressure and its relationship to diseases.

The sphygmomanometer that doctors use today was invented in 1896 by the Italian physician **Scipione Riva-Rocci**. It consists of a flexible hollow cuff that is wrapped around the arm. The cuff is inflated until the air pressure inside it matches the blood pressure in the patient's arm. As the cuff deflates, the doctor listens to the beat of the pulse while the blood pressure is read from a dial.

Because of the sphygmomanometer, doctors now know that high blood pressure, which doctors call hypertension, can be an indication of more-serious problems. Hypertension accelerates other diseases, overworks the heart muscle, and is a factor in strokes and heart attacks. Low blood pressure can also be an indication of serious health problems.

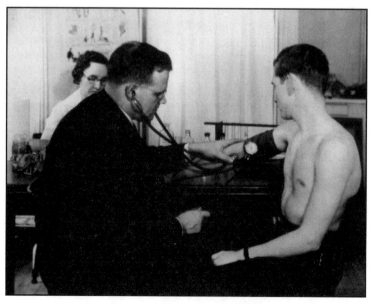

A Doctor Taking Blood Pressure

Tooth decay has been a common problem for people throughout history. It is important to halt tooth decay quickly and prevent more-serious conditions such as abcesses, infections in the mouth that can spread throughout the body and can ultimately prove fatal. The dental drill is an essential tool in halting this process, because it allows cavities in the teeth to be completely cleared of bacteria.

Historically, doctors dealth with tooth decay by simply extracting (pulling out) the damaged tooth, an operation that took place for many centuries without the use of anesthetics (see no. 20). False teeth were often put into the empty spaces. The Romans wore false teeth made of gold or ivory, and such teeth have also been found in the jaws of Egyptian mummies buried around 500 B.C.

The first metal fillings were inserted by English surgeons in 1673. French surgeon Pierre Fauchard (1678–1761), known as the father of modern dentistry, also developed the use of metal fillings. His book *The Surgeon Dentist, A Treatise on Teeth*, published in 1728, described some methods for removing decay and restoring teeth, and the filling of cavities with tin, lead or gold.

The regular practice of filling cavities began in the 19th century. For many years, thin gold foil or sponge gold was used. Other metals were used experimentally, but they were not acceptable substitutes for gold, which was easily worked into the damaged tooth and did not cause an allergic reaction in the body, as did some other metals. Gold's softness sometimes caused trouble, though, because pure gold fill-

A Foot Operated Drill

ings often had to be replaced. In 1826 dentists began to use "amalgams," the combination of one or more metals with mercury. These fillings were a great improvement because they were easily worked as gold, and were both durable and affordable, allowing more pat-ients to have their teeth repaired rather than pulled out.

With the advent of better filling materials, the need for a more effective drill became clear. Dentists had already experimented with various types of drills that operated by turning a handle. For example, President George Washington's dentist, John Greenwood, used a mechanism that he had modified from his mother's spinning wheel. To operate the drill, he tapped a foot petal.

It was in England in 1864 that the first motor-driven dental drill was invented by **George Fellows Harrington**. His drill was attached to a clockwork device held by the dentist. It was awkward, but it was an important beginning. Other motor-driven drills followed. In 1875 in Kalamazoo, Michigan, inventor **George F. Green** patented an electric dental drill, but his model was too clumsy and too heavy for general use. The leading reformer in American dentistry was **Greene Vardiman Black** (1831–1915). Black invented a foot-controlled motor that allowed the dentist to keep both hands free while using the drill.

More than 75 years later, in 1957, a high-speed dental drill was devised by **John V. Borden** in Washington, D.C. This new drill greatly reduced the time it took to repair patients' teeth, making dental health even more affordable. By 1971, it was in common use by dentists everywhere.

31. Antiseptics
1865

Ignaz **Semmelweis** introduced the concept of personal hygiene in hospitals by enforcing hand washing in 1847 (see no. 22). Although he was unable to convince some hospital authorities of the need to ensure sterile conditions, his theories were proved in 1865 by British surgeon **Joseph Jackson Lister** (1827–1912).

Lister had read **Louis Pasteur**'s theories about germs (see no. 27) and he understood that germs (bacteria) are what cause wounds to become infected. Lister was always careful when he operated, but no matter how large or small the surgery, at least half of all his patients died of blood poisoning when infections from the surgical wounds spread into the bloodstream. Lister had been studying the problem, and he noticed that when the patients in the wards had broken arms or legs, but no open wounds, they did not develop

infections. However, if the skin was broken, their wounds did become infected.

Previously, the development of pus and fever were believed to be caused by the weather and by "evil smells" in the air. After reading Pasteur's work, Lister began to experiment with disinfectants. His first experiment took place on August 12, 1865, on a man with a compound fracture, which is a fracture in which the injured bone is visible through the broken skin. Lister sterilized the wound with carbolic acid (phenol), a toxic byproduct of coal tar that has antiseptic properties, and the patient healed successfully. After that, Lister not only dabbed wounds with carbolic acid, but he also washed all of his instruments as well as his hands in the antiseptic, too. He even sprayed a fine mist of carbolic acid in the air to kill germs. His next experiment was also successful. He began using antiseptics while in surgery to prevent infections from starting, and the death rate of his patients dropped dramatically.

Reports of Lister's work spread, and soon surgeons were visiting him to observe and learn about his new antiseptics. Gradually, doctors learned that germs do not come from the air but from other sources like the dirt in the wounds, dirty instruments, the hands of the surgeons, and unclean bandages. Physicians began to focus on removvnig these sources of contamination, and and in 1886, the American company Johnson & Johnson introduced the first ready-to-use sterile surgical dressings. **Robert Wood Johnson** had heard Lister speak in 1876 and had developed sterile dressings wrapped in individual sealed packages.

Research continued, and doctors soon found better antiseptics that did not burn the patients' skin. Common antiseptics used today include isopropyl alcohol, compounds of chlorine and iodine, and silver nitrate, which is used to protect the eyes of newborn infants against gonorrheal infection.

Joseph Lister

32. Genetics
1865

Gregor Johann Mendel (1822–1884), an Austrian abbot living at a monastery in Czechoslovakia, became interested in **Rudolf Virchow**'s theories about the division of cells (see no. 28). Mendel began to conduct experiments on garden peas, planting 34 different kinds of pea plants and carefully noting the heights of the stalks, the shapes of the seeds, and the colors of the flowers and seeds. He fertilized each flower by hand and noted details about the plant that the resulting seeds grew into.

By keeping a careful record of his results, Mendel was able to determine which traits were likely to appear in the next generation of pea plants (the "dominant traits") and which ones were likely not to recur (the "recessive traits"). He also found that when he cross-fertilized two plants that had ancestors with a particular recessive trait, the seedlings they produced might have that recessive trait, too. For example, two tall plants with short ancestors might still produce a short plant, even though generally the trait for tallness was the dominant trait.

Mendel summarized his findings in two laws. He first theorized that through the sex cells — the ovum and the sperm, in humans — traits are transferred as separate and distinct units form one generation to the next. This theory is called "the principle of segregation." Mendel's second law, called "the principle of independent assortment," stated that traits are inherited independently of one another. Therefore, the trait of tallness may be inherited with any other traits, dominant or recessive.

Mendel stated that each inherited trait is determined by two hereditary factors, or genes: one from each parent. In the traits that he studied, Mendel found that one of the two genes always predominated over the other. For example, tallness was always dominant over shortness. This is known as "the law of dominance."

Gregor Johann Mendel

Ignored during his lifetime, Mendel's research was later rediscovered by three separate investigators, Dutch botanist **Hugo De Vries** (1848–1935), German botanist **Karl Erich Correns** (1864–1933), and Austrian botanist **Erich Tschermak–von Seysenegg** (1871–1962). The three botanists had each discovered Mendel's writings and replicated his findings. The laws were publicized in 1900, with all three botanists declaring Mendel as the discoverer of the process of heredity. Mendel's work has become the basic doctrine of **genetics**, a term that was coined by the English zoologist **William Bateson** (1861–1926) to describe the "physiology of descent."

Today, the Mendelian system is often explained in humans by using eye color as an example. Brown eyes are a dominant trait, while blue eyes are a recessive trait. This means that brown-eyed parents always produce brown-eyed children, unless both parents have blue-eyed ancestors. In that case, the gene for blue eyes can be passed down for many generations, hidden in the genes, until the child receives a gene for blue eyes from each parent.

33. The Medical Thermometer
1866

Before the invention of the medical **thermometer**, an instrument used to measure the temperature of the body, doctors checked for a fever simply by feeling their patients' foreheads. This method is not very accurate!

The first thermometer was invented by the Italian scientist **Galileo Galilei** (1564–1642) in 1593. He used it to measure changes in air temperature. His friend, the Italian professor **Santorio Santorius** (1561–1636), used Galileo's work as the basis of a crude clinical thermometer. Santorius' thermometer was the first to be used to measure the temperature of the human body. Santorius explained, "The patient grasps the bulb or breathes upon it into a hood, or takes the bulb into his mouth, so that we can tell if the patient be better or worse [sic], so as not to be led astray in knowledge of prognosis or cure."

Santorius had marked his thermometer into equal units between the temperature of snow

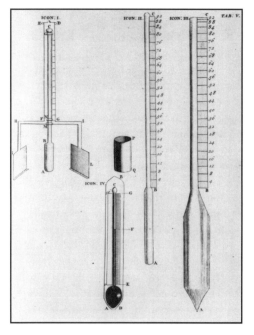

A Fahrenheit Thermometer

and that of a candle flame. The intent was not to measure the "normal" temperature of all human bodies, but to check the variations in temperature in one patient when well and when sick. As with Santorius' invention to measure the pulse (see no.11), this thermometer was not widely used in medicine. It was simply too large and too awkward to use easily.

It wasn't until 1709 that German physicist **Gabriel Daniel Fahrenheit** (1686–1736) invented the alcohol thermometer. His thermometer featured a scale that gave the normal human body temperature as 98.6°, the freezing point of water as 32° and water's boiling point as 212°. In 1714, Fahrenheit replaced the alcohol in his thermometer with mercury, which provides a a more accurate reading because it expands evenly when heated.

Over the next 150 years, several other thermometers and temperature scales were developed, including the Celsius and Reaumur scales. In 1866, English physician **Thomas Clifford Allbutt** (1836–1925) invented a clinical thermometer that was only six inches long and fit easily into the patient's mouth. After German physician **Carl Wunderlich** (1815–1877) established that fever is a symptom of some diseases, not a disease in itself, the thermometer became a valuable tool. With an accurate tool to measure body temperature, doctors could quickly determine whether or not there was a fever. Since the symptoms of some diseases are very similar, determining that a fever is present helps doctors arrive at an accurate diagnosis and devise better treatment plans.

Modern thermometers include small glass thermometers similar to Allbutt's, plastic strips that can be held to the forehead, electronic thermometers that are put into the patient's ear for only a few seconds, and even small plastic thermometers that are used once and then thrown away.

34. Cancer
1867

A **cancer** is a group of normal cells that for unknown reasons begins to grow too much, free from the body's natural systems of control. Sometimes the cells spread to other parts of the body, crowding out and killing normal tissue. For centuries, doctors could diagnose cancer, recognizing the uncontrolled growth of tumors, but they could do little to help their patients. The first written reference to cancer was in the *al-Tasrif (Collection),* compiled at Cordova, Spain, in A.D. 986. In this book,

Wilhelm Waldeyer-Hartz

the surgeon **Albucasis** (also called Abul Kasim) discussed all of Arabian medical knowledge; one of the diseases he described was cancer of the thyroid gland.

Nearly 800 years later, in 1761, London physician **John Hill** (1707–1775) reported six cases of cancer that were caused by the use of snuff, a tobacco-based powder that is inhaled through the nose. This was the first time a particular substance (in this case, tobacco) was linked to cancer. English physician **Thomas Hodgkin** (1798–1866) later described cancer of the lymph nodes, now called Hodgkin's disease.

However, the actual cause of cancer was not understood until **Wilhelm Waldeyer-Hartz** (1836–1921), a German scientist, wrote in 1867 that cancer is formed when cell division (see no. 28) becomes uncontrolled. He realized that cancer cells can spread to other parts of the body, initiating new growths, and that the only hope of curing cancer is to diagnose it and begin treatment at an early stage. It wasn't until the 20th century, however, that any real progress was made

toward curing cancer. In 1903 German surgeon **Georg Clems Perthes** (1869–1927) discovered that x-rays (see no. 43) can inhibit tumors and other cancerous growths.

In 1915, Japanese researcher **Katsusaburo Yamagiwa** (1863–1930) and his colleague **Koichi Ichikawa** began the first experiments to produce cancer in animals. By painting rabbits' ears with coal tar, they caused cancer to form. After further animal experiments, repeating their original success, they proved that the coal tar was the cause of the cancer.

British biochemist **Ernest Kennaway** (1881–1958) isolated the first cancer-causing chemical, or carcinogen , in 1933. He showed that certain organic compounds — chemicals composed mostly of carbon and oxygen — cause cancer in animals. Carcinogens are found in cigarette smoke, auto exhaust, and various types of pollution, among other sources. Further research linked smoking to lung cancer; excessive radioation to childhood leukemia, thyroid cancer and birth defects; and genetic factors to cancers of the breast and stomach.

Cancer research has come a long way, but there is still more work to be done. Both patients and doctors now understand the significance of the early warning signs of cancer. With the development of chemotherapy (see no. 60) and radiation therapy (see no. 55), cancer patients have a much greater survival rate. New treatments such as bone marrow transplants (see no. 91) and gene therapy (see no. 97) have been developed and are still being researched.

35. Tissue Grafting
c. 1869

Tissue grafting is the process of using skin or other tissues from another part of the body or from a donor to repair wounds caused by burns, injuries, or birth defects. The first human tissue graft was performed by Swiss surgeon **Jacques Reverdin** (1842–1929) in 1869. Reverdin implanted small slivers of skin into spaces made in the damaged tissue with a knife. From these tiny grafts, the skin gradually grew and spread, eventually covering the whole surface of the damaged area.

Through his experiments, Reverdin found that when skin is grafted from one part of the body to another on the same patient, or from one identical twin to another, the graft heals well. However, if the skin is taken from a donor and grafted onto another patient, the graft is usually rejected, becoming red, then blackening and dropping off within a few days. Reverdin's work paved the way for modern plastic surgery, although his patients risked death because there were no effective medications to prevent infections. Plastic surgery was first employed on a large scale to repair and reconstruct injuries suffered by soldiers in World War I. With the development of antibiotics (see no. 70), surgery became less dangerous, and it was common to repair birth defects and to reconstruct tissue disfigured by severe burns.

After World War II, British surgeon **Peter Brian Medawar** (1915–1987) began to study skin grafts. He discovered that the success of a graft depended on the familial relation between the donor and the recipient. Skin from a parent or sibling was more likely to be

Peter Brian Medawar

successful than that of a distant cousin or an anonymous donor. By 1953, Medawar had discovered that if he injected mouse embryos with tissue cells from unrelated adult mice, the newborn mice could later successfully receive skin grafts from the older mice. Since their immature immune systems had received and integrated the foreign cells while the ba-by mice were still developing, their bodies accepted the skin grafts without reacting to the foreign tissues. This acquired immunological response led to further research on anti-rejection techniques in organ transplants (see nos. 74 and 89).

When a skin graft is done today, usually to replace skin that has been destroyed by severe burns, large sections of skin are cut from other areas of the patient's body, or from a donor, and placed in the area where new skin must grow. This is usually done with a **split-thickness graft**, in which the skin is cut thinly enough that the tissue fluids at the recipient site will be able to nourish it, while enough living tissue is left in the original cut so that it can heal. Another procedure, called a **skin-flap graft**, works in a similar way except that the cut is made right next to the wound so that the skin graft can remain connected to the area of the cut, maintaining the blood supply to its new location in the damaged area.

Modern doctors have developed artificial skin to use when large amounts of skin is needed to cover injuries due to serious burns (see no. 95). Using artificial skin, they are able to save burn victims who otherwise would have died.

36. Leprosy
1873

Leprosy has been known since Biblical times and occurs most often in tropical countries. Most adults are immune to the disease, but about ten percent of the adult population is vulnerable, as well as most children. It affects the skin and nerves, and its victims develop sores and ulcers that disfigure their bodies, and many are crippled by the disease. In some regions, leprosy is a common cause of blindness and the major cause of loss of function in the hands. The disease is communicable through the mucous of the nose or throat, and usually takes between two and seven years to develop.

Leprosy came to England in 1230, when crusaders returned from their pilgrimages to the Christian Holy Land, in what is now Israel. It spread slowly, and many patients did not know where they had contracted the disease because victims do not develop symptoms for several years after infection. People believed that leprosy was both contagious (spread through contact with an infected person) and hereditary (spread from parents to their offspring through the genes). Since leprosy is not easily transmitted, it was very difficult for early doctors to trace the true agent, a bacteria, from one patient to another. There was no cure for this frightening and debilitating disease, so victims were often exiled or ostracized by society.

Since the disease often affected several people in the same family, researchers in recent times still believed that it is hereditary. However, the Norwegian physician **Armauer Gerhard Henrik Hansen** (1841–1912) had begun to study the disease in 1868 and noted in case histories that when family members were apart, the disease did not occur in the absent members. Hansen began searching for the bacteria, and in 1873 he identified *Mycobacterium leprae*. He never proved that this was the bacteria that causes leprosy (in fact, this mysterious bacteria is impossible to grow in a laboratory and only occurs within living animals), but he did convince doctors that the disease is contagious and that leprosy victims should be isolated. Leprosy is now sometimes called **Hansen's disease** because of Hansen's influential work.

Due to Hansen's efforts, leper colonies were established for the unfortunate victims. **Father Damien** (1840–1889) a Belgian Roman Catholic missionary, dedicated his life to helping patients at a large leper colony on Molokai, Hawaii. He administered to the lepers' spiritual needs, dressed their sores, provided shelter and food, and buried them when they died. He contracted the disease and eventually died of it.

Today, with the advent of sulfa drugs (see no. 67), leprosy can be cured, although patients must endure a long regime of treatment with antibacterial drugs such as dapsone. However, the disease still exists in Southeast Asia, Africa and South America, affecting ten to 15 million people worldwide.

The Leper Colony on Molokai, Hawaii

37. Brain Surgery
1879

Brain surgeries of various types have been carried out since prehistoric times. The first operations, called trephining, involved drilling a hole into the patient's skull, to allow the escape of "evil spirits" that caused sickness. Other early surgeons performed this operation to relieve pressure caused by swelling of the brain. Scientists know that some patients did recover from these primitive surgeries because skulls have been found in which the trephining holes had healed.

The brain was first associated with the central nervous system as early as 300 B.C. by the Greek physician **Herophilus of Chalcedon** (see no. 5). He dissected 600 human bodies and wrote about anatomy and other subjects. Herophilus' greatest contribution to medicine was demonstrating that the brain is the center of the nervous system by tracing the nerves from the brain to the spinal cord (see no. 16).

In 1664, English physician **Thomas Willis** (1621–1675) gave the most comprehensive and correct account of the brain and nervous system up to that point in his book *Anatomy of the Brain*. Among other things, Willis established a system for classifying cranial nerves. In 1881, **Sir Charles Bell** (see no. 16) determined that each nerve cell carries either motor or sensory stimuli.

The Scottish surgeon **Sir William Macewen** (1848–1924) pioneered successful brain surgery in 1879. His success in treating patients suffering from brain abscesses (swollen, inflamed tissue) was followed by the work of English surgeon **Rickman John Godlee** (1849–1925), who performed the first operation to remove a brain tumor on November 25, 1884. (His patient died 28 days later of other causes.) German physiologist **Friedrich Goltz** (1834–1902) began studying brain function soon afterwards. He experimented on dogs, and in 1892 he found that when the entire brain was removed, all functions except reflexes were lost.

William Macewen *(seated)* **With His Colleagues**

As surgeons began operating on the human brain, they found that certain portions of the brain had specific functions. This was first observed by English surgeon **Wilder Graves Penfield** (1891–1976) during operations on patients who suffered from an unusual type of seizure that brought on vivid hallucinations (visions that appear to be real) of previously experienced events. Penfield found that their hallucinations could be reproduced by stimulating a specific spot on the brain's surface. British neurologist **John Hughlings Jackson** (1835–1911) also studied seizures, muscle spasms and speech defects due to epilepsy and brain damage.

Another pioneer in neurosurgery, American surgeon **Harvey Williams Cushing** (1869–1939) (see no. 61), developed many techniques for brain and spinal cord surgery. As knowledge of the brain and its functions increased, surgeons were able to repair more-serious injuries and to remove tumors. New technology like the CAT scan (see no. 88) and MRI (see no. 93) assist modern brain surgeons, allowing them to map the areas of the brain where they will be operating.

44

38. Vaccinations
1881

Vaccination is the inoculation of a person or animal with a weakened or dead bacteria or virus. This procedure allows the body to manufacture natural defenses against the disease, so that it becomes immune. By the late 19th century, a vaccination technique for smallpox had been in use for almost 100 years (see no. 15). However, no one knew what the vaccine did or why it worked. Doctors learned one important clue when they discovered bacteria under the microscope, and recognized the relationship between bacteria and infection. After his theory that "germs" cause diseases was accepted by the medical community (see no. 27), **Louis Pasteur** continued to research this relationship, as did **Robert Koch**, who would identify the specific strains of bacteria that cause tuberculosis (see no. 39), cholera (see no. 25) and anthrax, an infectious and often fatal disease caused by the *Bacillus anthracis* bacteria. Pasteur, Koch, and other researchers soon began to try and develop vaccines for these and other diseases.

Pasteur began with experiments on chickens infected with cholera. He found that if he injected the birds with an actively growing bacteria culture, they died. However, if he gave them an old culture, in which the bacteria had weakened and died, the birds survived. Later, when he exposed the vaccinated birds to the live cholera bacteria, they did not become ill. They had become immune to cholera. Pasteur then began to experiment with the anthrax bacteria. Again, he found that if he injected cows with the dead bacteria, then later with a live culture, they were not affected by the disease.

Basing his research upon his vaccines for cholera and anthrax, in 1881 Pasteur began studying rabies. He could not find a bacteria for it, because it is not caused by a bacteria but by a virus, and viruses are too small to be seen under a microscope. However, Pasteur was determined to develop a vaccine against rabies, a terrifying and fatal disease that was common in the region of France where he grew up.

Pasteur traced the path of infection in animals from the saliva, to the nerves, to the brain, where it causes convulsions, madness, paralysis, coma and then death. He experimented with dogs, first injecting them with a weakened virus and then exposing the vaccinated animals to a rabid dog. His vaccine was successful.

In 1885, a desperate mother brought her nine-year-old son to Pasteur. The boy had been bitten 14 times by a rabid dog. Since the boy was certain to die otherwise, Pasteur took a risk and inoculated him with the rabies vaccine. It was the first test of the rabies vaccine on humans. The boy recieved ten injections, and he developed an immunity to the disease before it was able to take hold in his body. Then a young shepherd was brought to Pasteur who had also been bitten by a rabid dog. He was given the vaccinations, and he too survived. After that, patients flocked to Pasteur for help. More than 2,500 people were inoculated with the rabies vaccine in the following 15 months.

The victory against rabies spurred further research into vaccinations and immunology. By the 20th century, children were regularly immunized against such diseases as diptheria, measles, poliomyelitis, and tuberculosis.

Children Lined Up for Vaccinations

German bacteriologist **Robert Koch** (1843–1910) did important research that led to the development of vaccines by **Louis Pasteur** (see nos. 27 and 37) and other scientists. In 1877, Koch demonstrated a new technique for preparing bacteria for viewing under the microscope (see no. 9) using special dyes that made them easier to see. Koch's technique provided Pasteur with the information he needed to develop the vaccine for anthrax.

In 1882, Koch identified the bacteria that causes **tuberculosis**, *Mycobacterium tuberculosis,* and proved that the disease is contagious. Before the discovery of this bacteria, doctors believed that tuberculosis — also known as TB or consumption — was caused by weakened health or was hereditary. Tuberculosis usually

Robert Koch

affects the lungs, where it causes hard "tubercules" or nodules to grow, but other parts of the body can also be infected, including the intestines and joints. The disease is normally spread by inhalation, but it can also be spread through contaminated foods like unpasteurized milk and utensils. Symptoms include fever, weakness, loss of appetite, and coughing. Until modern times, tuberculosis was a major cause of death in Europe and North America.

Koch worked diligently on a vaccine for tuberculosis, but he was unsuccessful. Although he worked with the cultured bacteria as Pasteur had done with anthrax, it didn't work to prevent tuberculosis. However, once it was understood how the disease was spread,

doctors began to promote ways of avoiding it. Public information campaigns to discourage sneezing and coughing close to other people and forbidding spitting in public places helped to reduce the spread of the disease.

In 1891, the Koch Institute for Infectious Diseases opened in Berlin. Research on tuberculosis continued there. However, it wasn't until 1944 that **Selman Abraham Waksman** (1888–1973) and his colleagues isolated an antibiotic (see no. 70) that was could fight the disease. This antibiotic, streptomycin, was derived from a soil microbe and proved to be effective against the tuberculosis bacteria. In 1952 a more effective drug, isoniazid (eyeso-NIE-ah-zid), was finally developed. However, like many others, these drugs have side effects that are sometimes dangerous. They can cause dizziness and severe damage to the kidneys, as well as allergic reactions. Therefore, there is a continuing search for new and better drugs. Furthermore, some strains of the disease have begun to develop resistance to drugs because people fail to take their medication after they feel better. A vaccine was eventually developed, but it is not entirely effective.

Other bacteria Koch would identify include those that cause conjunctivitis, an infection causing inflammation of the eye (1883), and cholera (1884). Koch also studied sleeping sickness (see no. 51), malaria (see no. 45) and bubonic plague (see no. 40).

White Blood Cells
1892

While **Edward Jenner** and **Louis Pasteur** had developed vaccines for such diseases as smallpox and rabies (see nos. 15 and 37), no one really understood how vaccination worked. It was understood that the diseases were caused by "germs" (bacteria or viruses) and that patients who were inoculated with a small dose of the germs would become immune to them. However, the actual mechanism by which the vaccine helps the body to fight off the invading germs was unknown. Researchers continued to do research on this process at the Pasteur Institute in France.

Red blood cells had been discovered in 1658 by Dutch naturalist **Jan Swammerdam** (see no. 53), and had been viewed by **Anton van Leeuwenhoek** under his microscope (see no. 9). In 1892, Russian biologist **Elie Metchnikoff** (1845–1916), the director of the Pasteur Institute, presented the theory that there were other, special, amoeba-like blood cells in the body that attack the invading germs. These **white blood cells**, or leukocytes, play an important part in the vaccine's ability to immunize against a disease, he said.

Metchnikoff came to the conclusion that the white blood cells surround and destroy the foreign substances. The white blood cells produce antibodies that can work to disable the germs. When a patient is vaccinated, the body is exposed to the weakened or dead bacteria or virus, and it builds up antibodies against those specific germs. Then, when the patient is again exposed to the germs, the body can quickly fight them off. In 1908, Metchnikoff shared a Nobel Prize for his discovery.

Later research showed that there are actually three types of white blood cells: granulocytes, lymphocytes, and monocytes. The granulocytes, which are formed in the bone marrow, locate bacteria in the body and engulf them. The lymphocytes are produced mostly in the spleen and in the lymph nodes; they make the antibodies, which are different kinds of proteins that have a strong chemical attraction to specific bacteria or viruses. Thus, when patients receive the rabies vaccine, their white blood cells produce antibodies which are specifically attracted to the rabies virus. Antibodies attach themselves to the surface of the virus, making it easier for the granulocytes to engulf and destroy the virus. Monocytes are believed to originate from the lymphocytes. Monocytes attack the remaining organisms that are not destroyed by the granulocytes and lymphocytes.

There are usually only one or two white blood cells for every 1,000 red blood cells. However, when an infection occurs, the white blood cells dramatically increase in number to fight the invading microbes.

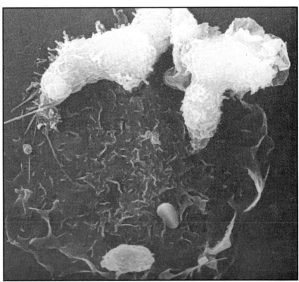

White Blood Cells

41. The Bubonic Plague
1894

Like smallpox, **bubonic plague** (known as the Black Death) has killed many millions of people through the ages. In the past, many people believed that it was spread mainly through the air. They formed this mistaken impression because it was easily transmitted in cities due to crowded living conditions. Although the Indian doctor **Susrata** (see no. 2) had noted the link between bubonic plague and rats in 750 B.C., this link was unknown to Western medicine for centuries. In fact, the disease is carried by the fleas on infected rats. Only after a human is infected from a rat flea can the disease be transmitted from person to person through the air. Its victims suffer chills, fever, vomiting, diarrhea, swollen lymph nodes, and finally, death.

As early as A.D. 125, various types of epidemics swept across North Africa, then made their way to Italy and further into Europe. In A.D. 541, the Great Plague of Justinian, which is believed to have been bubonic plague, spread from Egypt to Palestine to Constantinople (now Istanbul, Turkey) and throughout the Roman-Byzantine world. As many as 5,000 to 10,000 people died each day in Constantinople.

It is believed that this epidemic killed 100 million people in the Middle East, Europe, and Asia.

Bubonic plague spread across Europe again in 1348, killing 75 million people — about half the population — by 1350. A quarantine station was set up in Ragusa, Yugoslavia, in 1377, where people thought to have the plague were placed for 40 days so they would not spread it.

In the 1880s, with the discovery of bacteria and the success of the smallpox and rabies vaccines to guide him, Japanese researcher **Shibasaburo Kitasato** (1852–1931), a pupil of **Robert Koch** (see no. 39), began looking for the bacteria that causes bubonic plague. In 1894 both he and French researcher **Alexandre Yersin** (1863–1943), a pupil of **Louis Pasteur** (see no. 38) independently described *Yersinia pestis,* the plague bacteria, while studying an outbreak of plague in China. However, a successful vaccine was never made. Although the bacteria had been identified, there was still no effective treatment. Doctors could only try to make their patients comfortable and hope for the best. Epidemics of bubonic plague still spread across the European and Asian continents.

A vaccine for plague was developed in 1901, but it is not 100 percent effective and only lasts for a period of months. Since the discovery of antibiotics (see no 70) that can treat the disease, the death rate has dropped, but plague outbreaks still occur in nearly every part of the world. The common use of public health practices (see no. 19) has done much to reduce the incidence of plague. Since the initial infection is caused by fleas that spread the disease from infected rats, pest control has become the main preventive measure.

Examination of Rats for Bubonic Plague

Psychoanalysis
1895

Psychoanalysis is a process for revealing the subconscious motivations of an individual by inducing the person to speak openly about their real-life experiences and dreams.

Throughout history, patients with psychiatric problems were generally ostracized, isolated, or put into asylums. By the 1800s, reformers had come to the conclusion that psychiatric patients were often mistreated in the asylums. Although the care of the patients in such asylums did eventually improve, restorative psychological treatments were not commonly practiced until the end of the 19th century.

In 1882, the Viennese physician **Josef Breuer** (1842–1925) found that hypnosis, combined with thorough discussions with the patient, was effective in treating a girl suffering from severe hysteria (outbreaks of wild, uncontrollable feelings). Hypnosis allowed the girl to relive incidents involving her sick father. By discussing and examining her experiences, she was cured of her symptoms. Breuer told his colleague **Sigmund Freud** (1856–1939) about his patient and how he had cured her. Following in Breuer's footsteps, Freud experimented with hypnotism and with "talk therapy." In 1895, Freud and Breuer published the book *Hysteria,* which discussed their new "talking cure."

According to Freud, the symptoms of hysterical patients are rooted in forgotten and unresolved conflicts from childhood. He developed the methods of free association and dream interpretation for delving into the unconscious mind. Using free association, the patient would verbalize thoughts spontaneously as they arose, whether or not they made sense. In dream interpretation, the patients recorded their dreams and the analyst interpreted the meaning of the symbolic images.

Freud theorized that the human personality is divided into three parts: the id, the superego, and the ego. The id represents the child within,

Sigmund Freud

the subconscious. It is concerned with instinct, instant gratification and pleasure. The superego represents societal and personal control mechanisms. The ego is the conscious self and acts as the mediator between the id and the superego, balancing the demands of real life with the desires of the individual.

These theories were first met with hostility by other researchers studying the mind and its processes, but eventually they influenced all of 20th-century psychology. Later psychologists who disputed some of Freud's theories, like **Carl Jung** from Switzerland (1875–1961) and **Alfred Adler** from Austria (1870–1937), still based much of their work on Freud's.

Psychologists still use many of Freud's theories today. However, they are also aware that biological and social factors are also very important influences in many cases of mental illness. Therefore, modern treatment may include behavior therapy and drugs (see no. 73) as well as psychotherapy.

43. X-rays
1895

X-rays are a part of the spectrum of electromagnetic radiation Visible light and radio waves are also forms of electromagnetic radiation, but they have longer wavelengths and are not as powerful as x-rays. X-rays are among the most powerful forms of electromagenetic radiation, and their very short wavelenths allow them to pass through some forms of matter without being blocked.

In 1895, German physicist **Wilhelm Konrad Roentgen**, (1845–1923) discovered x-rays while conducting an experiment in which he sent electric currents through a glass tube. Every time he conducted the experiment, a piece of photographic paper lying covered up on a nearby table would change as though it had been exposed to light. Roentgen realized that invisible light rays were penetrating the cover and hitting the photographic paper. He tested these unknown rays, which he called x-rays, finding that they could pass through cardboard, thick books, wood, and rubber — but not lead. Over a period of several weeks, Roentgen took many x-ray photographs by placing various objects between the x-ray source and some film. One such photograph was of his wife's hand. Her finger bones showed clearly on the photograph, while her wedding ring showed up as a dark band because the x-rays had not penetrated the ring.

Continuing the research on x-rays were the French physicists **Pierre Curie** (1859–1906) and **Marie Curie** (1867– 1934). They are best known for their discovery of the element radium and the study of radioactivity. In 1906, Pierre died tragically in an accident in Paris. After his death, Marie threw herself into her work, and she dedicated the rest of her life to the study of radioactive materials and their medical applications. She concentrated on developing the practical use of x-rays in medicine. In 1914, Marie and her daughter, **Irène Joliot-Curie** (1897– 1956), established x-ray stations on the battlefields of World War I and used x-rays to help diagnose wounded soldiers. In 1918, Marie became the director of the scientific department of the Radium Institute. She died of leukemia on July 4, 1934, probably because of her long exposure to radiation.

In 1926 American biologist **Hermann Joseph Muller** (1890–1967) discovered that overexposure to x-rays creates mutations, or changes in the genetic structure of cells, which sometimes cause cancer. Because of his work, modern radiologists are careful to use x-rays at the lowest levels possible. On the other hand, **radiation therapy** (see no. 55) uses x-rays to destroy some forms of cancer. X-rays have become a very important diagnostic tool in medicine, allowing doctors to examine bones, blood vessels and other parts of the body. For example, in angiography (x-ray examinations of the heart and blood vessels), the doctor injects into the bloodstream a special liquid that x-rays do not penetrate. Using x-ray pictures, doctors can then track the liquid as it moves throughout the body and can see blockages and abnormalities in the blood flow.

Pierre and Marie Curie With Their Daughter Irene

44. Immunization
1897

In 1897, Polish bacteriologist **Paul Ehrlich** (1854–1915) presented the principle of "selective toxicity." He developed this theory while he was working at the Koch Institute doing research on vaccines (see no. 38). According to his theory, if a harmful substance, or toxin, is introduced into the body, the body automatically produces antitoxins or antibodies (see no. 38), which circulate in the blood and destroy the toxin. Therefore, he said, the body can produce an antitoxin, a type of anitbody that works against the toxin but is harmless to the body's own tissues and cells.

Ehrlich's theory was based upon the work bacteriologists **Emil von Behring** from Germany (1854–1917) and **Shibasaburo Kitasato** from Japan (1852–1931). These researchers were studying the way certain bacteria produce harmful substances in the body. In 1890 they made the first tetanus antitoxin. Tetanus is an often-fatal disease of the nervous system characterized by severe muscle spasms and convulsions. It is caused by the toxins produced in the body by the activity of the bacteria *Clostridium tetani.*

Von Behring was also looking for a diphtheria antitoxin. Diphtheria is caused by the bacteria *Corynebacterium diphtheriae.* It infects the throat and produces a toxin that circulates in the bloodstream to the rest of the body. Diptheria symptoms include fever, sore throat, and swollen lymph nodes in the neck. As the toxin spreads it can cause breathing difficulties, heart failure, paralysis and sometimes death.

Paul Ehrlich

Von Behring's success was inconsistent until Ehrlich began working on the problem in 1891. The first experiments were too harmful to be done on humans. Ehrlich injected a horse with graduated doses of the diptheria toxin, increasing the amount of toxin with each injection. The horse's body produced an increasing number of diptheria antitoxins in response. Ehrlich then infected the horse with the diphtheria bacteria, but the horse did not develop diphtheria.

Ehrlich's first human test was on Christmas Eve in 1891, when he gave the diphtheria antitoxin to a dying child. A week later, after a series of inoculations, the child fully recovered from the disease. Ehrlich published his work on antibodies in 1897, and in 1908 he shared a Nobel Prize.

Ehrlich's work on antibodies added to the important work on vaccines that had been done by **Louis Pasteur**, **Robert Koch**, and others. Doctors were able to fight off diseases not only by attacking the bacteria themselves, but also by attacking the toxins that the bacteria produced. This understanding opened a new area in medicine, **immunology**, the study of the body's specific responses to foreign substances. It also laid the foundation for modern immunization programs. Once doctors understood the importance of building up antibodies in the blood with immunizations, they began promoting these important methods of **preventive medicine** (see no. 81).

Ehrlich continued his work in immunology and did important research on drugs that led to the field of chemotherapy (see no. 60).

The Indian physician **Susruta** (see no. 2) was the first to record the links between rats and bubonic plague (see no. 41) and between mosquitoes and **malaria**, a disease that causes severe fever. Malaria is in fact spread by mosquitoes, and it has plagued humankind for many centuries. In A.D. 95 a deadly form of malaria appeared in the farms outside Rome, Italy, driving the farmers out of the countryside and into the overcrowded city, and resulting in widespread famine. Recurring epidemics of malaria in the later years of the Roman Empire may also have played a part in the empire's decline.

Since mosquitoes are common in most tropical and semi-tropical climates, malaria can spread very rapidly in these areas. By the 1600s, the disease had spread northward as far as England. In 1619, a deadly form was carried to the Americas by African slaves taken to Jamestown, Virginia. Since there was no treatment for malaria, this caused great alarm in the colonies. However, a treatment was discovered in the 1630s, when Spanish missionaries in Peru discovered the Indian's use of quinine, an extract from the bark of the cinchona (sing-KOH-na) tree. Quinine was the only antimalarial drug there was until the 20th century.

Before 1880, malaria was believed to be caused by gases from swamps. (The word "malaria" means "bad air" in Italian.) This was logical, since the disease often occurred in swampy areas. However, in 1880 French army physician **Charles Louis Alphonse Laveran** (1845–1922) was examining the blood of a malaria patient and discovered a protozoan

Ronald Ross

(one-celled animal) parasite within it. After many years of researching the cause of malaria, in 1897, English physician **Ronald Ross** (1857–1932) discovered that the female *Anopheles* mosquito transmits the parasites into the bloodstream of the people and animals she bites. Ross had been looking into the possibility that mosquitoes might carry the disease, since they are common in swamps and reproduce in standing water, and he identified the parasite within the stomach of the mosquito. Because of his work, swamps where mosquitoes bred were drained, the use of window screens and mosquito netting was expanded, and the use of insecticides became widespread. Ross received a 1902 Nobel Prize for his discovery.

Today, malaria is still common in some areas and is still often fatal. It occurs mostly in tropical regions such as Africa, Central America, and Southeast Asia. It is estimated that there are 270 million new cases of malaria each year, and two million deaths. While some ethnic groups have developed genetic defenses to the disease, their genes for modified red blood cells put them at risk for such genetic disorders as sickle cell anemia and thalassemia.

Although some drugs have been found to treat malaria, the parasites are developing a resistance to them, which makes them ineffective. Researchers are working hard to develop a malaria vaccine, but because four different types of parasites cause malaria, it is very dificult. In the meantime, for cases that are resistant to modern antimalarial drugs, quinine has again become the drug of choice.

Typhoid or"typhoid fever" is a severe, highly contagious infection caused by the *Salmonella typhosa* bacteria. Its victims suffer from a high fever and develop rose-colored spots on the abdomen and chest, as well as diarrhea or constipation. The disease is usually spread through contaminated food, water or milk.

The first recorded description of typhoid appeared in 1659 and was written by English physician **Thomas Willis** (see nos. 16 and 36). During the Crimean War (1853–1856), one of a series of wars between Russia and Turkey, more soldiers died of typhoid than from the battle. It was during this war that the English nurse **Florence Nightingale** (1820–1910) organized a military barracks hospital. She introduced strict standards of hygiene (see nos. 22 and 31) that greatly reduced the death rate of the soldiers. Still, infectious diseases like typhoid, cholera (see no. 25), dysentery and typhus (see no. 58) were rampant. Typhoid continued to take the lives of both the rich and the poor during the 1860s and 1870s. Epidemics of typhus, yellow fever, smallpox, scarlet fever, and cholera also raged in Baltimore, Boston, Memphis, New Orleans, New York, Philadelphia and Washington, D.C. during those years.

It was in 1880 that the typhoid bacteria was identified by German bacteriologist **Karl Joseph Eberth** (1835–1926) and by **Robert Koch** (see no. 39). By 1898, British pathologist **Almroth Edward Wright** (1861–1947) had developed and used an anti-typhoid vaccine. Wright took very virulent forms of the bacteria, killed them with heat, then injected them into his patients in two doses, ten days apart. His system was extremely effective. During World War I (1914 –1918) only 100 soldiers died of typhoid.

In 1903 a series of typhoid outbreaks began in New York that resulted in more than 1,300 cases of the disease. The epidemic was finally traced to **Mary Mallon** (1870?– 1938), who became known as "**Typhoid Mary.**" She was a cook who carried the disease without suffering any visible symptoms. She was imprisoned in 1907 for handling food while knowingly carrying the disease, but when released she again resumed working as a cook, this time under an assumed name. She refused to believe that she was responsible for the typhoid outbreaks, despite having been tested and proven to be a carrier. Finally in 1915, after health officials again found her serving food, she was isolated on an island for the rest of her life. She never cooperated with doctors, refusing all treatments. She is believed to have infected at least 53 people and caused three deaths.

By 1921, many states had begun instituting laws that promoted good dairy practices, improving the safety of milk. Since milk is now normally pasteurized (see no. 27) and food service workers are required to wash their hands after using the toilet, cases of typhoid have become rare in the U.S. Doctors now treat typhoid with **antibiotics** (see no. 70).

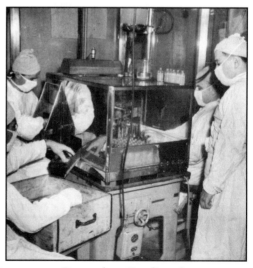

Researchers Bottling the Typhoid Vaccine

47. Aspirin
1899

Over the centuires, people have believed that various plants can cure illnesses (see no. 1). For example, hemp, mistletoe and the juice of the poppy flower were thought to "drive away" the "evil spirits" of pain. The fresh buds of hemlock trees were thought to cure scurvy (see no. 12), and the aches and pains of arthritis (also see no. 72) were eased by the bark of willow and black birch trees.

In 1763, English clergymember **Edward Stone** reported that the bark of willow trees was "very efficacious in curing aguish [intense fever] and intermitting disorders [bouts of fever]." Stone had first discovered the remedy while out walking. He had absentmindedly pulled off a piece of willow bark and chewed it, and then noticed its effects. Stone tested the folk remedy on himself for five years, noting that it relieved his arthritis.

In the 1830s, the anesthetic substance that Stone had discovered, the chemical compound **salicylic acid,** was isolated from another plant, the meadowsweet. Like the willow bark, the meadowsweet extract indeed relieved pain; however, it was so strong that most people couldn't tolerate the stomach irritation it caused. French chemist **Carl Frederick Gerhardt** (1833–1902) first synthesized **acetylsalicylic acid**, or **aspirin,** in 1853. His process of manufacturing aspirin was too time-consuming to be practical as a drug: It would not have been cost-effective to produce enough aspirin for general consumption. However, German researchers **Felix Hoffmann** and **Heinrich Dresser** soon perfected a new and easier method of preparation.

While working as a chemist for the drug company **Bayer** in 1899, Hoffmann began researching better methods of producing the painkiller. In the laboratory, a new chemical was developed from coal tar. With Dresser, his colleague, Hoffmann experimented with the new formula and found that it relieved his father's arthritis symptoms without the stomach irritation caused by the old medication. Dresser and Hoffmann's formula was less irritating to the stomach because they added a buffering substance that helped neutralize the acid in the stomach. Bayer patented the formula and marketed it as Bayer Aspirin. It was available by prescription beginning in 1905. Aspirin pills are now consumed literally by the billion.

Aspirin's chief drawback is that it still has a tendency to irritate the lining of the stomach of some users, sometimes causing bleeding. In large doses, aspirin is toxic and can cause kidney damage. Aspirin should never be given to children with viral diseases; this usage has been associated with **Reyes syndrome**, a rare and often fatal disease.

Today, it is known that aspirin not only lowers fever and relieves headache, muscle pain, and joint pain but also reduces inflammation, especially that of rheumatic fever and arthritis. It has also been found to inhibit the formation of blood clots, so it is used in low doses to prevent heart attacks and strokes. New over-the-counter anti-inflamatory painkillers have been developed, including ibuprofen and acetaminophen, but for many doctors and patients, aspirin remains the best remedy for pain.

A Box of Bayer Aspirin

Yellow fever is an infectious disease caused by a virus that is transmitted through mosquito bites. It's called "yellow fever" because one of the symptoms is jaundice, a yellowing of the skin and eyes due to liver damage. Other symptoms include fever, chills, and in severe cases, internal bleeding, coma and death. The disease is found throughout tropical and subtropical regions.

The first reliable record of yellow fever appeared in western medical literature in 1635 after the disease broke out on Guadeloupe and St. Kitts islands in the Caribbean. Another outbreak swept across the Yucatán Peninsula in Mexico in 1648. Like **malaria** (see no. 45), it was believed that yellow fever was caused by swamp gases and "bad air."

Walter Reed

In 1881, Cuban-American physician **Carlos Juan Finlay** (1833–1915) suggested that mosquitos might transmit yellow fever. Only one year later he identified the *Aëdes aegypti* mosquito as the most likely carrier. Finlay tried to prove this theory for the next 19 years. However, his experiments were not controlled properly, and he failed. In 1900, a U.S. Army surgeon named **Walter Reed** (1851–1902) initiated experiments on yellow fever. It was urgent that Reed identify the source of the disease, as there was an outbreak of it among the U.S. soldiers in Cuba. During their first experiment, two of Reed's researchers were bitten by mosquitoes that had previously bitten yellow fever victims. Although one of the researchers died, this fact did not prove that it was the mosquitoes that carried the disease because there was no control group; that is, an unexposed group that otherwise did the same activities as the men who had been infected. Therefore, the researchers couldn't be certain that it was the mosquitoes, rather than some other unknown factor, which had caused the yellow fever.

In the second group of experiments, Reed used hospital tents to separate the volunteers. The group that was protected from mosquitoes remained disease-free. However, the other group that was exposed to the mosquitoes caught yellow fever. Once the carrier was identified this way, **Major William C. Gorgas** (1854–1920) of the U.S. Public Health Service began mosquito-control efforts in Havana. He ordered that all pools of standing water be drained so the mosquitos couldn't breed, and he had a thin layer of oil applied over swamp water to kill the mosquito larvae. By 1901, Havana was nearly free of the disease.

In 1904, Gorgas was sent to Panama. The U.S. government wanted to build a canal across the isthmus, but previous efforts by the French had failed because so many laborers had died, many of yellow fever and malaria. The U.S. was determined to build the canal because of the economic and strategic benefits it would bring. Gorgas' mosquito-eradication program was so successful that the U.S. War Department began building the Panama Canal in 1906 and completed it in 1914.

Researchers also began working on a vaccine for the yellow fever virus. **Max Theiler** (1899–1972) a South African–born American microbiologist, won a Nobel Prize in 1951 for developing a yellow fever vaccine.

Joining Blood Vessels
1902

While many medical milestones — such as the development of the smallpox vaccine or the invention of the microscope (see nos. 5 and 9) — are obviously giant steps in medicine, others are small steps that lead to huge results. The work of French surgeon and experimental biologist **Alexis Carrel** (1873–1944) is an example. His simple innovation of stitching blood vessels together led to such medical miracles as organ transplants (see nos. 74 and 89).

Carrel spent much of his career in the U.S., experimenting in surgery. In 1902, he developed a new method of suturing cut blood vessels back together, end to end, using very fine needles and thread. This allowed both blood vessels and organs to be grafted together during surgery. Before Carrel's technique was developed, surgeons could not reconnect most of the tiny blood vessels, so they were unable to perform very complicated surgeries like transplanting organs, which are usually surrounded by many delicate blood vessels. If the blood vessels are not carefully sewn together when the new organ is inserted during a transplant, the organ will not receive enough blood to nourish it, and it will die from lack of oxygen and nutrients. Carrel's new method solved this problem. It was so important to medicine that he received a 1912 Nobel Prize for his techniques.

After World War I, Carrel resumed his research on vascular suturing and the grafting of blood vessels and organs. Among his many experiments, he performed successful heart surgery on a dog in 1914. In 1936, he collaborated with **Charles Lindbergh** (1902–1974), the famous American aviator, in inventing an artificial heart (see no. 92). He used this new invention to keep different kinds of tissues and organs alive by keeping oxygenated blood moving through them.

Once there was a method of keeping the organs alive, researchers could study them further, increasing their knowledge about the various organs. With this new ability and knowledge, along with Carrel's earlier techniques of suturing blood vessels, other researchers could begin to experiment with organ transplants. Without Carrel's work, the kidney transplants, heart transplants and other surgeries that are frequently performed today would be unthinkable.

Alexis Carrel

56

Blood transfusions were first performed in the 17th century. They were very dangerous, however, because the donors' blood sometimes caused the recipients' blood to clot, causing severe illness and death. The reason the blood clotted was not known. In 1900, Austrian pathologist **Karl Landsteiner** (1868–1943) began investigating .

By 1902, Landsteiner found that different kinds of human blood could be identified in the laboratory according to the presence or absence of certain chemicals, called "antigens," which are located on the surface of the red blood cells. He determined that human blood has four different types: O, A, B and AB. The antigens on A, B, and AB form antibodies (see no. 44) when injected into a patient. Because these antibodies can be dangerous to the patient receiving the blood transfusion, the blood type of a donor must be the same as the blood type of the patient. The exceptions to the rule of A-to-A or B-to-B transfusions are found with the blood types O and AB. Since type O does not have antigens, it is universal, and can be given to anyone. AB blood can receive any of the other three types, since it already has the antigens of both A and B. Landsteiner received a Nobel Prize in medicine in 1930 for his discovery of blood types.

Although the existence of blood types had been established, there were still problems with some transfusions. Landsteiner continued his research in immunology and the chemistry of antigens. It wasn't until 1940, however, that he and two colleagues, **Alexander Wiener** and **Philip Levine**, identified the Rh factor. The Rh factor is a protein found on 85 percent of people's red blood cells, and it is designated as either positive or negative.

When Rh-positive blood is given to an Rh-negative person, the Rh-negative person develops antibodies to the foreign Rh factor.

Dr. Karl Landsteiner

A serious or fatal reaction may occur if the two blood types are later mixed; for example, if the patient receives several transfusions.

Once doctors learned about blood types and the Rh factor, all blood transfusions could be done safely. In 1940, New York surgeon **Charles Richard Drew** (1904–1950) opened the first blood bank. He had developed a way of preserving blood plasma, the liquid part of blood used in transfusions. During World War II, he was the director of the first American Red Cross Blood Bank. He also headed the program that sent blood to Great Britain for the wounded soldiers there. Sadly, Drew was not allowed to donate his own blood because he was African-American. The racist attitudes of the era did not allow the mixing of blood from people of different races. Fortunatley, the world today has outgrown this idea, and people now understand that the only important considerations regarding blood transfusions are Landsteiners discoveries — blood types and the Rh factor.

According to historical accounts, sleeping sickness has existed in Africa for centuries. In the first written accounts of the disease by **Khaldun**, a 14th-century Arab traveler, it was noted that the chief of one tribe spent most of his time sleeping, and died after two years. Like many other victims of the disease, the chief may have died of starvation, since the extreme lethargy caused by sleeping sickness suppresses the appetite. However, the disease also slowly damages the central nervous system over the years, so it may have been nerve damage that caused his death.

Sleeping sickness was not a major concern to Europeans until the 1800s, because until then the disease had been isolated to the area south of the Sahara desert. As travel to Africa increased, however, the incidence of the disease in Europe also increased. In 1902, the British government sent out a group to study sleeping sickness. The Italian doctor **Aldo Castellani** (1874–1971), an expert in tropical diseases, performed autopsies on a number of victims. He discovered that many of the victims had a previously unknown parasite in their brains. When British doctor **Sir David Bruce**

Sir David Bruce

(1855–1931) joined the group, he and Castellani compared their findings. Previously, Bruce had studied a disease called "nagana," which affects cows. He had discovered that nagana was caused by the *Trypanosoma* parasite and that it was transmitted by the bite of the tsetse (SET-see) fly. When the two men collaborated, they discovered that they were looking at two parasites that are closely related.

Although they had discovered the cause of sleeping sickness, the doctors still had to devise a way to avoid infection. Bruce mapped out areas where the tsetse fly was common and recommended that travelers avoid those areas. It wasn't until the 1920s that the German drug company Bayer introduced an **arsenic** compound to kill the parasite that an effective medicine was available. Since arsenic is a highly toxic substance, the amount of medicine prescribed must be carefully measured so it is enough to kill the parasite without harming the patient.

There are more than 100 **parasitic diseases**, and many of them have been observed and recorded since ancient times. The three major groups of parasites are protozoans, helminths, and arthropods. Protozoal parasites are one-celled creatures that usually infect the bloodstream and body tissues through the bite of mosquitoes and flies or through contact with contaminated water or food. These parasites include amoebas, flagellates, ciliates and sporozoans.

The group of helminths include flukes, tapeworms and roundworms. Arthropods include ticks, mites, lice and fleas. A few examples of diseases caused or carried by these organisims include amoebic dysentery (severe diarrhea), malaria (see no. 45), toxoplasmosis and typhus (see no. 58). Parasitic diseases remain dangerous in many parts of the world, especially to children, who are the most vulnerable.

Hormones are chemicals that move through the body and regulate many bodily functions. They control such things as growth and development, metabolic rate, and reproduction. The proper amount of hormones is maintained in the body by mechanisms that rely upon the interactions between the glands that produce the hormones, the other organs, and the blood.

Many diseases are caused by lack of or insufficient amounts of certain hormones in the body. One example is goiter, enlargement of the thyroid that is associated with low levels of thyroid hormone and a sluggish metabolism. Diabetes, which is caused by lack of insulin or improper use of insulin in the body (see no. 62), causes serious complications in the body and can be fatal. Certain types of infertility can be caused by an imbalance of the sexual hormones. Since many hormones act together in the body, rising and falling in relation to each other, an imbalance of one hormone can sometimes set off a cascade of other imbalances.

As important as hormones are, before the 20th century they were essentially unknown. In 1893, British scientists **Edward Schäfer** and **George Oliver** injected a dog with an xtract from the adrenal gland. The animal's blood pressure skyrocketed, indicating to the scientists one function of the adrenal gland, which later became known as adrenaline. In 1901, the American researcher **Jokichi Takamine** (1854–1922) isolated adrenaline. It was the first hormone to be isolated.

In 1902, English researchers **Sir William Maddock Bayliss** (1860–1924) and **Ernest Starling** (1866–1927) began experimenting with the duodenum, a part of the small intestine. They injected the duodenum of a living dog with hydrochloric acid and found that the dog's pancreas began to secrete digestive juices. The two scientists reasoned that there must be some substance that originated from the duodenum, traveled through the bloodstream, and

Ernest Starling

caused the pancreas to react. They called this substance "secretin." It wasn't long before they realized that there are other substances, the other hormones, that also travel in the blood and cause reactions in other organs.

Bayliss and Starling continued their work, finding that secretin also acts on the liver when the contents of the stomach enter the duodenum, increasing the flow of pancreatic secretions. By 1905 they had figured out that the nervous system does not directly control the chemical coordination of these functions.

Since these discoveries, scientists have found that there are basically two kinds of hormones: peptides, or chains of amino acids; and lipids, which include steroids. The main glands that produce hormones are the pituitary (see no. 61), the thyroid, the parathyroid, the adrenal gland, and the thymus, as well as the pineal gland, the pancreas, the ovaries and the testes. Since serious disorders are caused by the lack of any hormone, many hormones are now synthesized for use in treating deficiencies. Among these is the growth hormone somatropin, which was first synthesized in 1971. It has great potential for helping children who are dwarfed by a lack of the natural hormone, which is produced by the pituitary gland.

53. Chromosomes
1902

Chromosomes are the carriers of genetic traits (see no 32). The number of chromosomes that exists in every organism differs from one species to another. There are 46 paired chromosomes in the nucleus of every human cell.

In human reproduction, the sex cells (the ovum and sperm) each contain half of the paired set of chromosomes — like one side of an unzipped zipper. When the ovum is fertilized by the sperm, the zygote that forms contains one set of single chromosomes from each parent, forming a complete set of pairs (like zipping up the zipper). One of these pairs of chromosomes contains the genes that determine the sex of the baby. A pair of x chromosomes results in a female, and an x-and-y pair results in a male. (Each egg contains an x, and each sperm contains either an x or a y, so there are never two y's).

The concept of chromosomes was first postulated by French mathematician, physicist, and biologist **Pierre Louis Moreau de Maupertuis** (1698–1759) in his book *Système de la Nature* in 1751. He theorized that the human embryo goes through several different stages of development, rather than being pre-formed and simply growing larger. He observed that offspring reveal characteristics of both parents, a fact well known to animal breeders. He also pointed out that previous theories could not explain the recurrence of six-fingered hands in one Berlin family nor explain the rare instances of "albinism," the lack of pigmentation in human skin.

Although the work of **Gregor Mendel** (see no. 32) showed that various traits are carried down from parents to offspring, researchers still did not understand the mechanism that caused this to happen. Some suspected that chromosomes played a part in heredity, but it wasn't until American researcher **Walter Sutton** (1877–1916) began to study Kansas grasshoppers in 1902 that the relationship between chromosomes and Mendel's theories became clear. He created detailed studies of grasshopper chromosomes, showing the various phases of grasshopper development, including the egg, the larval stage, and the adult stage. He determined that all chromosomes exist in pairs, with an organism's offspring receiving one set of chromosomes from each parent.

Meanwhile, in Munich, Germany, **Theodor Boveri** (1862–1915) came to the same conclusion as Sutton. Boveri was working with the eggs of the roundworm when he proved that specific chromosomes were responsible for specific characteristics in the roundworm's offspring.

Later researchers discovered that chromosomes also determine the sex of the offspring, and they pinpointed the location of genes in the chromosomes of the cell nucleus.

Chromosomes of Normal Male

In 1830, Italian researcher **Carlo Matteucci** showed that the heart muscle generates an electrical pulse as it works. In 1887, English physiologist **Augustus Volney Waller** (1816–1870) performed an experiment to measure his heartbeat using an electrometer, a device consisting of a column of mercury in a glass tube that was immersed in a solution of diluted sulfuric acid. When Waller stood with each foot in a basin filled with salt solution and connected to the poles of the electrometer, the electrical action of his heart caused the mercury to move within the tube in time with his pulse. One witness to this demonstration was Dutch physiologist **Willem Einthoven** (1860–1927).

In 1903, Einthoven invented the string galvanometer. His instrument consisted of a coil of fine wire that was attached to a magnet. An electric current was passed through the coil, which then became magnetized, causing the poles of the magnet to coil to repel each other and moving an attached pointer across a calibrated scale. Einthoven placed the galvanometer near the heart, and as the heart beat, the electric current it produced magnetized the coil and moved the pointer. Its position was then recorded on a photographic plate.

Einthoven used this information to track variations in the heartbeats of his patients. He later defined the meaning of the changes in the heart's patterns of electric current. He learned what was a normal heartbeat, and linked abnormal readings with specific kinds of heart disease. In 1924, Einthoven was awarded a Nobel Prize for his invention.

Einthoven's simple string galvanometer was later developed into a more sophisticated machine, the **electrocardiograph** (EKG), which is an invaluable tool in medicine. Using an EKG, doctors can measure deviations in the normal height, form, and duration of the wave patterns that illustrate the heart's electric pulses on a screen. As Einthoven discovered, these changes can indicate specific disorders; thus, the EKG is an important aid in diagnosing many diseases of the heart. EKGs can also be taken while the patient is exercising, revealing differences between the oxygen levels in the blood supply and demonstrating the heart muscle's oxygen requirements. By taking an EKG of patients under stress, doctors can see if the circulatory system (see no. 8) is able to meet the heart's increasing demand for oxygen as it works harder. This information can indicate the liklihood of a heart attack.

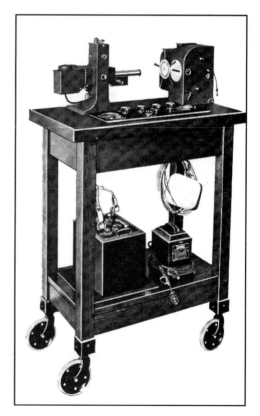

The Sanborn Electrocardiograph

55. Radiation Therapy
1903

In 1903, German surgeon **George Clems Perthes** (1869–1927) made the first discovery that x-rays (see no. 43) sometimes inhibit cancer. He had exposed a tumor to x-rays and found that not only had the tumor stopped growing, but it actually got smaller. Perthes' research led to the invention of machines that could beam radiation onto cancers. These early machines, however, could only beam radiation a few inches into the body, so they were ineffective with tumors located deep within the body unless the patient was exposed to massive doses of radiation, which sometimes meant the treatment cured one cancer but caused another.

Early **radiation therapy**, also called "radiotherapy," used the element radium, which was discovered by **Pierre and Marie Curie** (see no. 43). Today, cancerous tumors are exposed to a radioactive element called cobalt 60. This method is safer for the patient.

Despite **Hermann Joseph Muller**'s discovery in 1926 that overexposure to x-rays could cause genetic mutations (see no. 43), it took many years for researchers to realize that radiation of any kind could be dangerous. During the testing of atomic bombs in the 1940s and 1950s, soldiers close to the bomb sites were exposed to very high levels of radiation and suffered aftereffects that ranged from mild to severe. Even consumers were frequently exposed to radiation. Shoe shops thought nothing of using x-rays to see if a shoe fit, and doctors often x-rayed pregnant women to see how the baby was growing. It was not until 1956, when x-rays were linked to childhood cancers and birth defects, that doctors began warning against the excessive use of radiation and began to curb their own use of it.

Research has found that cancerous tissues are more sensitive to radiation than normal tissues are. If the cancer has not spread and is not surrounded by radiation-sensitive tissue, such as the spinal cord, it can often be treated with radiation. Coupled with new, sophisticated techniques like computer analysis, radiotherapy is very effective. Current radiotherapy can direct the radiation to an exact spot within the bones and organs of the body. Depending on the type of cancer, the therapist usually uses an external high-energy beam, directing it at the tumor site for a short time each day over two to six weeks. In another technique, a tiny piece of radoactive material is placed precisely next to the tumor. This is good for sensitive areas like the brain and the optic nerve.

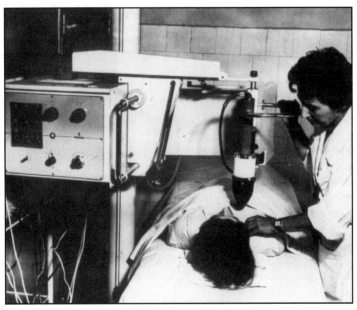

Radiation Treatment

Corneal Transplants
1906

Eye surgery to remove cataracts had been performed since 750 B.C. (see no. 2), but another frequent cause of blindness, damaged cornea, remained a problem for many centuries Today, the major cause of blindness in poor countries is the bacterial disease trachoma, which clouds the cornea. Caused by an infection of the bacteria *Chlamydia trachomatis,* trachoma affects more than 400 million people worldwide, particularly in Asia and Africa. Although antibiotics (see no. 70) are effective against this disease, once the eye is damaged, the only way to restore vision is to transplant a new cornea onto the victim's eye.

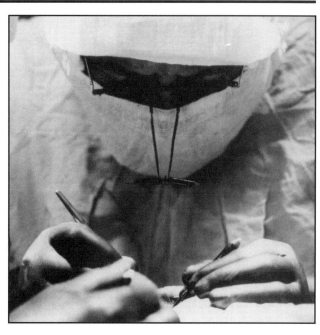

A Doctor Performs a Corneal Transplant Operation

The first known attempt to replace a cornea was performed in the early 1800s. While the operation, on a gazelle, was a success, further attempts failed. It was not until 1906 that a German surgeon, **Eduard Zirm** (1863–1944), successfully transplanted a human cornea onto the eye of a patient. It was an extremely delicate operation, and most surgeons who tried to duplicate Zirm's technique failed. However, very fine needles and silk thread became available after World War II, allowing the new cornea to be attached more accurately during surgery.

In the 1960s, doctors began using lasers in corneal transplants. The laser made the operation quicker and caused less scarring. By the 1990s, Zirm's once-unique feat became the most common transplant performed. The transplanted corneas usually come from recently deceased person who were willing to donate their organs to help others. Despite the success of corneal transplants, however, about ten percent of these operations result in the body rejecting the donor cornea. Anti-rejection drugs often don't work in the case of corneal transplants.

In 1997, American researcher **Jerry Niederkorn** announced a breakthrough technique in desensitizing the body to the donated cornea. Experiments in mice had found that, if skin cells from the donor were fed to the recipient ten times daily, the cornea was less likely to be rejected. This follows the common technique of giving animals and people the material that makes them react, thereby desensitizing the body's immune system (see nos. 41 and 59).

It is possible that in the near future, patients will swallow capsules containing cells from the donor before their transplant operation, thereby desensitizing their bodies to the new cornea.

Sir Frederick G. Hopkins

Vitamins are building blocks for the body. These nutrients, either natural occurring or synthesized, are necessary for the body to maintain good health. Other essential nutrients include carbohydrates, lipids, proteins, and minerals.

Vitamins play an important role in metabolism, which is the process cells go through to assimilate food and break down waste matter. However, vitamins are not generally made within the body. They come mainly from food. The exceptions are vitamin D, which is made within the body to a limited extent, and vitamin B12, which is made by beneficial bacteria in the intestinal tract.

Until the discovery of a cure for scurvy (see no. 12), the role of vitamins was essentially unknown. Even then, the specific element within the citrus fruits that cured scurvy remained a mystery. It wasn't until 1906, when British biochemist **Sir Frederick Gowland Hopkins** (1861–1947) experimented with rats, that it was shown that a diet had to include "accessory food items," later known as vitamins, for the rats to thrive. Hopkins fed two groups of young rats a diet of salts, sugar, starch, lard and protein. The first group also received small amounts of milk. They thrived. The second group, however, received no milk and did not grow. This led Hopkins to his breakthrough observation that there was some minute substance in the milk that helped the rats to grow.

Hopkins continued in his research, but he never identified the precise agent that assisted the body in using protein and energy to grow. Hopkins did share a 1929 Nobel Prize for demonstrating the existence of growth-promoting vitamins. The importance of his work was not realized until Polish-American biochemist **Casimir Funk** (1884–1967) stirred public interest with a paper on vitamin deficiency diseases in 1912. He called Hopkin's unknown elements "vitamine" and later theorized the existence of four vitamins: B1, B2, C and D.

Later researchers discovered that the disease known as rickets is not an infection but rather a result of lack of a vitamin. Rickets is a bone disease which deforms and disables children early in life. It is caused by a deficiency in vitamin D. American researcher **Elmer Verner McCollum** (1879–1967) isolated vitamin D in 1922 and used it to successfully treat rickets. He found that vitamin D plays a role in raising the amount of calcium and phosphate that is deposited in the bones.

In 1928, vitamin C was isolated from peppers at Cambridge, England. It was then identified as the vitamin within citrus fruits that prevents scurvy. By 1948, 13 main vitamins — A, B1, B2, B6, B12, C, D, E, and K — had been isolated. In the U.S., the Food and Nutrition Board was established and produced a brochure listing the **Recommended Dietary Allowances**, or RDA, of vitamins and other nutrients. These allowances are still used as a general guide for planning nutritionally balanced meals.

Typhus (TYE-fuss) is a parasitic disease (see no. 51) that comes in several forms, all caused by different strains of the *Rickettsia bacteria,* which is transmitted by fleas, lice or mites. The major symptoms of the disease are high fever, severe headache, depression, disorientation, delirium, and pink rashes that turn brown over time. The disease is also called "prison fever," "ship fever" and "typhus fever." Epidemic typhus is the most serious type. It is caused by the bacteria *Rickettsia prowazekii,* which lives only in humans and in body lice.

Typhus is associated with crowded, unsanitary conditions. As with many other diseases, military campaigns throughout history have been influenced by outbreaks of typhus. For example, in 1157 Frederick I's army at Rome was destroyed by a plague that most likely was typhus.

In 1892, American pathologist **Theobald Smith** (1859–1934) discovered that Texas cattle fever was spread by ticks. In 1903, French physician **Charles J.H. Nicolle** (1866–1936) was studying how typhus spreads from one person to another at the Pasteur Institute in Tunis, North Africa. He realized that, once patients were admitted to the hospital, they did not spread the disease to anyone else. Intrigued, he investigated the admission process. By this time, cleanliness and good hygiene had become very important in treating patients (see nos. 22 and 31). All patients were bathed and deloused, and their clothes were disinfected. Nicolle speculated that typhus might be transmitted by body lice, which were common at the time. He began experimenting and succeeded in transmitting typhus to guinea pigs, monkeys and other animals through lice. After Nicolle's findings were published in 1909, the public realized that it was important to stay free of lice in order to avoid diseases like typhus. Nicolle's work was a major advance in showing why clean and uncrowded living conditions were important to public health (also see nos. 10 and 19). He was awarded a Nobel Prize in 1928.

Although typhus has now become rare in the developed countries of the world, it still exists in many places where people live in crowded, dirty conditions such as those in refugee camps. Body lice are an ongoing problem in public health, since all forms of lice are easily spread through body contact, bedding, clothing, hats and hair brushes. Prevention by avoiding infestations with lice is the best solution to the problem, but there is now also a vaccination available for the kind of typhus that is spread through lice.

A Typhus Awareness Poster

An **allergy** is a reaction of the body to a substance that is normally harmless. The word "allergy" comes from Greek and means "abnormal response." People are often allergic to such mild irritants as pollen, mold, dust, certain foods, drugs, animal dander and insect stings. Allergic reactions may include hay fever (which includes of sneezing, watery eyes, or nasal congestion) from airborne allergies; rashes, upset stomach, or hives from food or drug allergies; and spasms within the lungs that interfere with breathing, when asthma occurs. Some people can have an extreme allergic reaction to certain allergens in bee or wasp stings, penicillin (see no. 64) or other drugs, or certain foods such as shellfish. This severe reaction, called anaphylaxis, can be life-threatening.

The earliest records of hay fever were made in 1565 by **Leonardo Botallo** (b. 1530). He called it "summer catarrh" and described how it occured in three men after they had smelled roses. However, the causes of the condition remained unknown until German doctor **Wilhelm Dunbar** (1863–1922) began to investigate. In 1903, he proved that airborne pollen is the culprit. Dunbar found that hay fever is actually caused by the body's release of a toxin in response to exposure to the irritating substances, called allergens. However, he was unsuccessful in his efforts to produce an antitoxin (see no. 44).

Finally, in 1910, English physiologist **Sir Henry Dale** (1875–1968) identified such a toxin, now called "ergotamine," when studying ergot. Ergot is a poisonous fungus, *Claviceps purpures,* which sometimes infects rye kernels. When it is eaten by livestock or humans, the fungus can cause hallucinations and occasionally fatal illnesses. During medieval times, epidemics of ergot were frequent in Europe.

It was another 16 years before Dunbar made the connection between histamine, a related toxin, and allergic reactions. This discovery revolutionized the study of allergies. When researchers knew what caused the reaction, they could search for substances to counteract it.

It was more than ten years before such a substance was developed. In 1937, a Swiss-Italian pharmacologist named **Daniele Bovet** (1907–1992) who was working at the Pasteur Institute finally developed the first medication, called an **antihistamine**, to block the release of histamines. Today, while antihistamines are somewhat effective against allergies, other treatments are also used. Anti-inflammatory agents such as corticosteroids (kor-ti-koh-STER-oids) are helpful in some allergic reactions, such as severe hives. Decon-gestants are also useful for a short time, but then they become counterproductive because the body becomes dependent upon them.

Avoiding the offending substance is the best solution to allergies, but this is not always practical. Many patients refuse to give away their beloved pets or forgo dust-catching items like book collections or carpets just because of their allergies.

Sir Henry Dale

60. Chemotherapy
1910

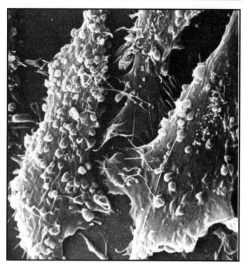

Cancer Cells

Chemotherapy is the use of chemicals that are not produced within the body to treat a disease in the body. **Cancer** (see no. 34) is the disease most often thought of when discussing chemotherapy. However, it was **Paul Ehrlich**'s work on immunology (see no. 44) that led to the development of chemotherapy. During his research, Ehrlich theorized that some substances could be used to attack only the harmful bacteria, the disease-causing organisms that were present in the body, while leaving the rest of the body unharmed. While using a staining technique to help identify microorganisms under a microscope, he discovered that a certain kind of dye kills the organism that causes sleeping sickness (see no. 51).

In 1910, Ehrlich developed the first antibacterial drug, compound number 606, which cured syphilis in mice. Syphilis is a sexually transmitted disease caused by the bacteria *Treponema pallidum*. It can damage the brain and spinal cord, the skin, and the bones, and can cause heart failure, miscarriage, birth defects and death. Ehrlich marketed the new drug under the name **Salvarsan**. It reduced the number of serious cases of syphilis in humans in England and France by 50 percent by 1915. In spite of the importance of the cure, it was attacked by critics, who felt that curing syphilis encouraged sexual promiscuity. However, the development of this drug marked the real beginnings of chemotherapy.

Researchers have been since then for a substance that would work the same way against cancer. The search has been long and difficult. Unlike syphilis, which is caused by one bacteria and can be treated with one medicine, cancer has many causes — many of them unknown — and it requires different treatment depending on what part of the body it has affected. Also, it is caused by the body's own cells, growing out of control. A drug that can kills cancer could also be harmful to the other cells.

Cancer can metastasize; that is, spread into the bloodstream and throughout the entire body. Once it has done this, both surgery and radiation therapy (see no. 55) are no longer effective. It becomes very important to kill the cancer cells throughout the body. So far, chemotherapy is the closest that researchers have come to finding a method for doing this, but patients must be monitored closely as the drugs are very strong and can be toxic. They often cause nausea, loss of appetite, and baldness. Chemotherapy drugs also depress the immune system, making patients very vulnerable to other diseases. Chemotherapy drugs are often administered in injections, but they can also be given in pill form; in either case, they require the close supervision of a doctor.

Although it is not always 100 percent effective, chemotherapy has increased the life spans of many cancer patients. It is most effective in treating cancer of the blood (leukemia), and cancer of the lymphatic system (lymphoses).

67

The **pituitary gland** is found at the base of the brain. Considered "the master gland," it controls growth, reproduction and the body's metabolism through the release of hormones (see no. 52). It is made up of a front section and a back section, called the anterior and posterior lobes. The anterior lobe secretes somatropin (also called "growth hormone"), which promotes body growth; prolactin, which stimulates the production of milk in nursing mothers; adrenocorticotropic hormone (ACTH), which stimulates the adrenal cortex, the outer part of the adrenal gland; thyroid stimulating hormone (TSH); and two gonadotropic hormones, follicle-stimulating hormone (FSH) and luteinizing hormone (LH). The last two control the function and maturing of the sex organs. (The posterior lobe of the pituitary also secretes two additional hormones.)

The anterior lobe of the pituitary also regulates the function of the six hormones listed above. Removing or destroying the pituitary gland stops body growth, inhibits milk secretion, and causes the adrenal glands, the thyroid gland, and the sex organs to shrink and stop

Dr. Harvey William Cushing

functioning. If this happens in childhood, the patient stops growing. On the other hand, excess secretion of pituitary hormones can cause gigantism as well as abnormalities in the function of the adrenal gland, the thyroid, and the sex organs.

Although it was known that the thyroid and pituitary glands secrete hormones (see no. 52), many of the functions of those hormones were unknown until 1908, when U.S. surgeon **Harvey Williams Cushing** (1869–1939) began studying the pituitary gland. He experimented on dogs, then he studied 50 human patients whose pituitary glands excreted either too much or too little of the growth hormones. He studied the hormone levels in each of these patients, evaluating the different amounts of hormones and their effect upon the patients. This showed that all the hormones are interlinked, working together within the body to regulate its functions. Cushing's book *The Pituitary Body and Its Disorders* was published in 1912. It marked the beginning of the science of endocrinology, the study of the endocrine system hormones and the glands that produce them.

One of the conditions that he described is now known as **Cushing's syndrome**. The symptoms of this syndrome include fatty deposits in the face, neck and abdomen, muscular weakness, and masculinization in women. It is caused by overactivity in the adrenal gland.

Years later, the Polish-American biochemist **Andrew V. Schally** (b. 1926) showed that the hypothalamus, the part of the brain that contains the pituitary gland, controls the pituitary through hormones. In 1969, Schally and French-American physiologist **Roger Guillemin** (b. 1924) independently discovered a hypothalamic hormone, thyrotropin-releasing hormone (TRH). Schally identified and synthesized other hypothalamic hormones and showed how they control pituitary functions.

Diabetes mellitus is a chronic disease in which the body either does not produce enough insulin or does not properly use it. Insulin is a hormone (see no. 52) produced in the pancreas that is used by the body to transport energy, in the form of sugar (glucose), from the bloodstream into the body's cells. Diabetes and its complications are the fourth-leading cause of death by disease in the U.S. Both genetics and the environment seem to be implicated in the development of the disease. It has no cure.

There are two major types of diabetes mellitus. The first is insulin-dependent, or type I, diabetes, in which the body produces very little or no insulin. It often begins in childhood or early adulthood. The other type is non-insulin-dependent, or type II, diabetes, in which the body over time stops producing enough insulin or can no longer use insulin. It is the most common form of the disease and is also known as adult-onset diabetes because more than 90 percent of cases appear in people over age 20. Complications of diabetes include blindness, the inability of wounds to heal properly, kidney failure, heart disease, and nervous system disorders. Some diabetics must take daily insulin injections to stay alive.

Diabetes was known at least as early as 1674, when Oxford University's **Thomas Willis** (1621–1675) wrote that the urine of diabetics was "wonderfully sweet as [if] it were imbued with Honey or Sugar." English physician **Thomas Cawley** recorded a diagnosis of diabetes mellitus in 1783 after demonstrating that a patient's urine contained sugar. (The patient's body was not able to use the sugar in the bloodstream, so it was eliminated in the urine.) In 1788 Cawley noted abnormalities in a diabetic patient's pancreas.

The French physician **Etienne Lancereaux** made the connection between diabetes and pancreatic disorders in 1860. In 1889, German physiologists **Joseph von Mering**

Frederick Banting and Charles Best

(1849–1908) and **Oskar Minkowski** (1858–1931) began an experiment by removing the pancreas of a dog. Although the animal survived the surgery, it urinated more frequently, and the urine attracted flies and wasps because of its high sugar content. The dog went into a coma and die. The researchers realized that understanding the role of the pancreas was the key to a treating diabetes.

The isolation of insulin from the pancreas of a dog in 1921 by Canadian medical researchers **Frederick Grant Banting** (1891–1941) and **Charles Herbert Best** (1899–1978) gave diabetics a new lease on life. They tested the hormone first on a dog and then by giving each other shots. In their first real test in humans, they used the extract to save the life of a 14-year-old boy who was dying in Toronto General Hospital.

In 1966, insulin became the first hormone to be synthesized in a laboratory. The two researchers licensed **Eli Lilly** to produce the first commercial insulin — the first treatment for diabetes other than diet restrictions.

63. Brain Waves
1924

Human beings have about 100 billion nerve cells in their nervous systems, most of them within the brain. Each brain cell is connected to between 5,000 and 50,000 other nerve cells. The nerve impulses are carried along as waves of electrical activity that can be measured on the scalp.

An electroencephalograph records the electrical activity of the brain. Electrodes are placed on the scalp and connected to the machine, which records the brain waves on a sheet of paper. The recording is called an electroencephalogram, or EEG.

It is not easy to interpret an EEG. The brain is very complex, and the electrical recording apparatus is unable to distinguish the direction of the waves within the brain. The activity and frequency of the waves also vary, depending on what part of the brain they occur in. How-ever, certain abnormal patterns are associated with conditions like brain tumors, epilepsy and strokes. A patient's EEG can assist in diagnosing these conditions. The EEG can also determine if a hospital patient is "brain dead" by showing whether or not there is any brain activity.

In 1874, the first record of brain waves was made by British doctor **Richard Caton**. He connected his measuring device directly to the brain of a rabbit.

In 1924, German psychiatrist **Hans Berger** (1873– 1941), excited about **Willem Einthoven's** work with the **electrocardiograph** (EKG) (see no. 54), decided to use a **string galvanometer** to record brain activity. First he tried it on a dog, exposing its brain and measuring the electrical currents. Then he attached electrodes to the brains of humans who had already had part of their skulls removed during surgery. After he refined his method, he was able to read brain activity with electrodes attached to the scalp. He used himself and his friends and family as test subjects in obtaining EEGs. He published his results, the first information about human brain waves, in 1929.

In 1935, the first studies in English onthe use of the EEG in diagnosing human epilepsy were published by **Frederic Gibbs, Hallowell Davis** (1896–1992), and **William G. Lennox** (d. 1966), of Harvard Medical School. Berger had identified two different kinds of brain activity, which he called alpha and beta waves, and in 1953 sleep researchers led by **Nathaniel Kleitman** discovered new kinds of brain activity in sleeping patients.

Today, doctors continue to use the EEG as an important tool. For example, brain waves are recorded during brain surgery (see no. 37) to help surgeons avoid essential areas of the brain, such as those that control sight, speech and movement.

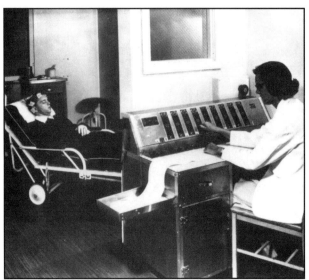

Reading Brain Waves on an EEG

Most medical milestones are arrived at through years of hard work and careful research. Yet one of the most important discoveries of the 20th century was a lucky mistake. **Penicillin** , the wonder drug that researchers had been looking for to cure all kinds of diseases, started out as an accidentally contaminated culture left in a petri dish while Scottish bacteriologist **Sir Alexander Fleming** (1881– 1955) went on vacation.

The understanding of antibiotics began with **Louis Pasteur**'s theory that one kind of bacteria can kill another, and with **Paul Ehrlich**'s work on selective toxicity (see nos. 37 and 44). Fleming took up the study and began searching for antibacterial substances during World War I. In 1921, he discovered lysozyme, an antibiotic enzyme that attacks many types of bacteria. The only problem was, it didn't kill any bacteria that caused diseases in humans.

Fleming continued his research, and the breakthrough finally occurred in 1928. Fleming had been studying *Staphylococci* (staf-uh-loh-KOK-sye) bacteria, which cause boils as well as infections in wounds, the heart and the blood vessels. He had been growing *Staph* cultures in petri dishes in his laboratory. In 1928, Fleming took a short vacation. Upon his return, he found a mold growing in some of the dishes. As he went to clean up, Fleming was astonished to notice that all the bacteria near the growing mold had been destroyed. The mold was *Penicillium,* a rare organism that was being grown in another laboratory that was downstairs from

Sir Alexander Fleming

Fleming's. Amazingly enough, however, Fleming failed to realize the implications of his historic discovery.

Because **penicillin** lost its strength when mixed with blood in a test tube, research into the drug stopped until 1940. After the outbreak of World War II, two bacteriologists read a paper that Fleming had written about penicillin. Australian researcher **Howard Florey** (1898–1968) and German researcher **Ernst Chain** (1906–1979), who were both working in England, joined forces and began to study penicillin. They isolated the chemical that was given off by the fungus, then tested it on four of the eight mice that they had injected with a fatal dose of another harmful bacteria, *Streptococci* (strep-tuh-KOK-sye). Within hours, only the four mice injected with penicillin were still alive.

Encouraged by their success, Florey and Chain soon began human trials. Penicillin quickly became known as a wonder drug — the first antibiotic — saving thousands of injured soldiers' lives. For their historic work, Florey and Chain shared a 1945 Nobel Prize with Fleming.

Today, many more antibiotics have been developed (see no. 70). However, they are not really "wonder drugs." Some antibiotics, like penicillin, can cause rashes, shock, or even death to the allergic patient. Another problem is that many antibiotics have become less effective as resistant strains of bacteria evolve. Because of the widespread use of antibiotics today, many bacteria are developing a resistance to these drugs.

An **iron lung** is a large metal chamber that a patient lies inside of, with his or her head remaining outside. A rubber collar is fitted tightly around the patient's neck, minimizing air leakage. Air pressure in the tank is decreased; the chest expands, and air is drawn into the lungs. Then the pressure in the tank is returned to normal, and the lungs release their air. By alternating between normal and low air pressures in the tank, the iron lung helps the patient to breathe for long periods of time.

The iron lung was the first mechanical device that could take over an essential function of the human body. It was invented by **Philip Drinker** of Harvard University in 1927. He improvised, using two vacuum cleaners and other old equipment to make his Drinker Respirator. It was used for the first time at Boston Children's Hospital in October 1928 to treat a child paralyzed by polio (see no. 77).

Polio can affect the patients' lungs and diaphragm, causing severe and permanent disability or death. Similar paralysis can also be caused by spinal cord injuries. Without the iron lung, patients with these problems would have quickly died.

Although the iron lung restored life to many victims of polio, their lives were often very different afterwards. **Lee Hale** of Crockett, Virginia, is known as the person who spent the longest period of time within an iron lung. After contracting polio in 1943 at the age of 32, Hale was paralysed from the neck down. He survived 32 years within an iron lung, at home and under the constant care of his wife. Because of his difficulty breathing, Hale ate only one meal per day, leaving his stomach empty the rest of the time to allow more space in his abdomen for breathing.

While the iron lung was widely used for only 20 years, its development led to modified forms of respirators, including the cuirass respirator, which surrounds only the chest and abdomen. A positive-pressure type of respirator was also developed. It acts by forcing air into the lungs and then letting the air escape. Yet another type is the demand, or assist, respirator, which is triggered by the user's drawing in of breath.

The importance of the invention of the iron lung and the more modern respirators is demonstrated every day. From assisting paralyzed patients to breathe, to supplying air-borne medications; and from helping workers avoid hazardous fumes, to supplying air to premature babies in a controlled environment, the respirator is essential to modern medicine.

A Patient in an Iron Lung

The Electron Microscope
1932

The **electron microscope** is a powerful tool based on the design of the standard light microscope (see no. 9). The electron microscope works in a similar manner as the light microscope; however, instead of directing a beam of light at a sample of tissue on a slide, it directs a beam of electrons *through* a very thin sample of tissue. It uses the extremely short wavelengths of accelerated electron beams — ejected from a "gun" that speeds up the electrons — to form precise images and resolve fine details. While a modern light microscope can magnify objects up to about 2,000 times their normal size, modern electron microscopes can magnify objects up to a million times.

German physicist and electrical engineer **Ernst August Friedrich Ruska** (1906–1988) and his colleague **Max Knoll** (1893–1969) built the first prototype of an electron microscope in 1931. It was capable of magnifying objects 17 times. The first practical model was built the following year, and the first commercial model appeared in 1935. By 1950, by refining the lens design and other technical features, engineers were able to make an electron microscope that magnified up to 20,000 times. For his work, Ruska shared a 1986 Nobel Prize in physics.

Using this new ability to view cells with a greater magnification and clarity, medical researchers were suddenly able to view tiny details of cells that they had been unable to see with light microscopes. Electron microscopes have vastly extended the range of details and the kinds of cell structures that can be observed. They are now used to study individual cell structures and large molecules. In medicine, they are used to look for abnormalities in cells, such as cancer, and to detect the presence of viruses, which are extremely small.

Ruska and Knoll's first electron microscope became known as the transmission electron

An Electron Microscope

microscope, or TEM. To use a TEM, the sample of tissue to be examined must be treated in several complicated ways. Most importantly, the sample must be sliced very thinly, so the electron beam can pass through it. For the scanning electron microscope, or SEM, which first gained wide use in the 1960s, the sample doesn't need to be as thin. This is because the electron beam is reflected off the sample, rather than passed through it. SEMs produce images that reveal the surface topography of the sample, rather than its inner structures.

Other types of modern electron microscopes are the scanning transmission electron microscope, or STEM, which combines the functions of the TEM and the SEM, and the scanning tunneling microscope, or STM, which has the advantage that samples need no initial preparation at all.

Sulfa Drugs
1935

Although it may be hard to imagine today, there was a time when a person could die from a sore throat. A simple infection like strep throat, caused by the *Streptococci* bacteria, was incurable. While penicillin (see no. 64) had been discovered in 1928, its usefulness against infections was not developed for many years.

The German physician and chemist **Gerhard Domagk** (1895–1964) noticed in 1932 that a particular red dye (which was later named Prontosil) killed *Streptococci* bacteria when he injected it into his laboratory mice. Since Prontosil had already been patented as a dye, he waited several years before publishing his findings; it is likely that he was searching for a similar chemical that

he could patent in his own name for use as a drug. In any case, in 1935 Domagk finally made his discovery public after using prontosil to save his daughter from death from a *Streptococcus* infection.

In the meantime, however, **Daniele Bovet** (see no. 59) at the Pasteur Institute had heard about Domagk's experiments on mice. He and other scientists tried the same experiment on humans and found that the drug worked fine. One problem, however, was that the dye turned the patients' skin bright red. After further research, Bovet's team found that the drug can be divided into two chemicals and that the active part, sulfanilamide (sul-fah-NILL-ah-mide), is colorless.

This breakthrough was amazing. Now, for the first time, doctors had a medicine that could actually save patients' lives by stopping an infection from developing further. While sulfanilmides, commonly called "**sulfa drugs**," don't kill the bacteria, they stop them from multiplying, thereby stopping the infection. Sulfa drugs were used against pneumonia and childbed fever (see no. 22), saving thousands of lives. For his discovery, Domagk was awarded a Nobel Prize in 1939, but the Nazi regime in Germany forced him to decline the prize for political reasons. His later work included research on tuberculosis and cancer drugs.

After the development of antibiotics (see no. 70), the use of sulfa drug in therapy became limited. They are still used, however, against streptococcal infections, urinary-tract infections and ulcerative colitis. Since some **bacteria** have become resistant to antibiotics in recent years, sulfa drugs are now being used more often.

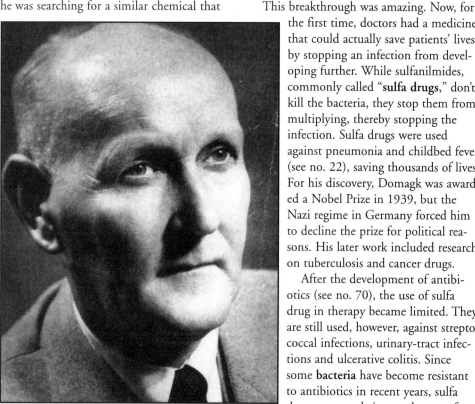

Gerhard Domagk

Plastic surgery, also known as reconstructive surgery, is the branch of surgery focused on correcting physical deformities and disfigurements caused by birth defects, injuries or disease. "Plastic" in this context refers to the idea that parts of the body can be molded or reshaped; what plastic surgery involves is a reshaping of parts of the body. It includes rebuilding lost or deformed ears, noses, or jaws; repairing cleft lip or cleft palate; reconstructing the body after surgery to remove cancer (see no. 34); repairing damage after burns; correcting birthmarks or scars; and inserting implants to give a normal appearance where some part may have been absent at birth — for example, a missing muscle.

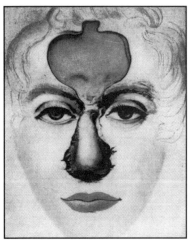

Eary Indian Method of Plastic Surgery

Another function of plastic surgery is purely cosmetic. Many people are dissatisfied with their appearances, perhaps thinking that their noses are too large or the skin under their eyes sags. Plastic surgery can sometimes help, but in many cases these individuals' psychological desire for changes in their appearances may be more important than the physical "improvements."

The practice of plastic surgery began as early as the **Gupta dynasty** of northern India in the fourth through sixth centuries. In 1597, Italian surgeon **Gasparo Tapliacossi** published the first textbook on early techniques of plastic surgery in Europe, which revived the practice of rhinoplasty, or nose surgery. However the actual science of plastic surgery began with the work of the Swiss surgeon **Jacques Reverdin** in 1894 (see no. 35).

His work on tissue grafting marked the beginning of the ability of surgeons to repair severe damage to the skin.

After World War I, there were many disfigured veterans. A large number had terrible facial injuries. **Sir Harold Gillies** (1882–1960), a British surgeon, started a plastic surgery unit to treat these veterans. His goal was to make the soldiers look as normal as possible. He hired New Zealand surgeon **Archibald Hector McIndoe** (1900–1960) as an assistant in 1932. McIndoe opened the Centre for Plastic and Jaw surgery in 1939, by which time he was well prepared for the influx of badly burned World War II air force soldiers.

When airplanes were shot down, the soldiers parachuted out, often falling through burning debris. The most common injuries of survivors were burns to their faces and hands. Because of the severity of the burns, the skin was completely destroyed in places, requiring extensive skin grafts and many operations. His patients, although grateful for his dedication, jokingly called themselves "The Guinea Pig Club" after one patient grumbled, "We're not fliers anymore. We're nothing but a plastic surgeon's guinea pigs." In the club were more than 600 members from 16 different countries.

McIndoe's work was so important to plastic surgery that many of the techniques he pioneered are still being used today to help other burn victims. In addition to skin grafts, he also worked with other forms of transplantation, including the grafting of bone, muscle, cartilage, tendons and nerves.

The two kidneys filter excess water, toxic wastes and other chemicals out of the blood and dispose of them in the urine. They maintain the balance of water in the body and the pH balance of the blood. When the kidneys do not function properly, or stop working altogether due to injury or acute or chronic diseases, impurities build up in the blood and poison the body. Eventually the patient dies. Diabetes mellitus (see no. 62) is the leading cause of kidney failure.

It was not until the 20th century, when doctors had developed a greater knowledge of the human body and how the various organs work and interact, that researchers began to try to find a way to remove impurities from the blood by using **dialysis**. Dialysis is the process of filtering the blood through membranes that allow certain dissolved substances to pass through them and prevent the passage of other substances.

John Jacob Abel

American researcher **John Jacob Abel** (1857–1938) and a team of scientists began working on an artificial kidney for a dog, and by 1913 they had succeeded in constructing such a device. Further development was delayed, however, by the lack of such things as a blood anticoagulant to keep the blood from clotting in the machine, a suitable membrane to filter the blood, and a delivery machine for the saline solution that would carry away the impurities.

After more than 30 years, in 1943, Dutch physician **Willem J. Kolff** (b. 1911) devised the first kidney machine for human patients. Since an operation was necessary to insert the machine's large tubes into an artery and a vein, the machine was used only for brief emergency treatments. The patient's blood flowed through tubes in the machine and was circulated on one side of a cellophane membrane, while a saline solution circulated on the other side. The waste products in the blood were drawn through the membrane in the process of osmosis and were carried away in the saline solution.

Many improvements on the original machine have been made since the 1940s. The saline solution bath has been replaced by a sophisticated machine that delivers a more efficient solution to the artificial organ. There are also a number of safety monitors to protect the patient. In 1955, the machine, now known as the dialysis machine, was made available as a presterilized and disposable unit. In addition, in 1960, U.S. physician **Belding Scribner** improved the kidney machine by developing a way to put tubes into the patient's artery and vein so that they can be left in place for months or even years. This simplified the treatment for patients with permanently damaged organs.

Antibiotics
1943

After the discovery and development of penicillin (see no. 64), researchers began searching for the next "wonder drug." French-American bacteriologist **Réne Dubos** (1901–1982) had been studying Pasteur's early work regarding germs (see no. 27). He noted that the bacterial populations in soil held one another in balance. By isolating and purifying various soil bacteria, he developed another antibiotic in 1939. This and several similar substances were very effective when Dubos applied them to superficial wounds, but they were toxic when ingested. However, during his work isolating such antibiotic substances as tyrocidine and gramicidine, Dubos established guidelines that were later adopted by his former teacher, Russian-American researcher **Selman Abraham Waksman** (1888–1973).

Waksman and several of his colleagues continued Dubos' work, and by 1943 they had isolated **streptomycin** from a soil microbe. The following year, they proved its effectiveness against the tuberculosis bacteria (see no. 39). For the first time, it was possible to cure victims of tuberculosis as well as bubonic plague. Mass production of both streptomycin and penicillin began during World War II. Because of the effectiveness of these antibiotics, many wounded soldiers avoided or were cured of infections, and thousands of lives were saved. For his momentous discovery, Waksman was awarded a Nobel Prize in 1952.

With the triumph of these new antibiotics, researchers were inspired to search for more and better medications. Between 1945 and 1960, a systematic search was made for bacteria and molds from all over the world that might have the potential of being the next antibiotic. Hundreds were discovered, and many were screened for antibiotic activity and

Selman Waksman

toxicity. Between 1960 and the 1990s, variations of natural bacteria and molds, designed in the laboratory, also became available. In addition, synthetic antibacterials have been developed. The successes of antibiotics against infections have resulted in tons of antibiotics being prescribed every year.

Unfortunately, the great success of antibiotics has also led to doctors to generally overprescribing these drugs. This overuse, coupled with the careless attitude of many patients (including not taking the entire dosage prescribed and thereby allowing some bacteria to survive), has resulted in bacteria becoming resistant to certain antibiotics. This is a major concern because some bacteria that can only be effectively destroyed by a few antibiotics are now becoming resistant to them, making these bacteria extremely dangerous. Another concern with the overuse of antibiotics is that some people can become sensitized to them, resulting in allergic reactions and making the drugs unsuitable for treating later infections.

71. Open Heart Surgery
1944

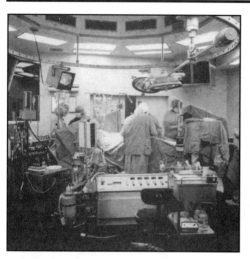

Open Heart Surgury

In 1893, U.S. surgeon **Daniel Hale Williams** (1858– 1931) performed the first open heart surgery in Chicago, Illinois. Heart surgery was done successfully in Germany in 1897 and 1924, and in England in 1913, 1925, 1931, and 1938. However, open heart surgery, a difficult and dangerous procedure that involves cutting into the heart itself, was a rare procedure for several more years, until doctors began to seek a cure for blue baby syndrome.

Blue baby syndrome occurs when birth defects in the circulatory system prevent blood from being pumped normally through the lungs. Since the blood does not reach the lungs, the baby's body gets unoxygenated blood, causing the blue skin color. Before open heart surgery was developed, blue babies normally died.

Helen Taussig (1898–1986), the head of the cardiac clinic at the Harriet Lane Home for chronically ill children, noticed that some blue babies lived longer than others. Upon investigation, it was found that the surviving babies all had the same unusual secondary defect — an open duct between the heart and the lungs. Normally this duct closes as the baby continues to grow after birth. However, Taussig realized that the duct was keeping some of the blue babies alive longer because it allowed their blood to become oxygenated.

In 1944, Taussig asked a surgeon at Johns Hopkins Medical School, **Alfred Blalock** (1899–1964), to perform open heart surgery and insert such a duct into a blue baby that was not born with this secondary defect. The operation, on a 15-month-old infant, took place on November 9, 1944, and was a success. This new procedure revolutionized open heart surgery, and by the time these infants had grown to be adults, open heart surgery had advanced to the point where they could have surgery again to completely correct their heart defects.

Later, American physician **Dickinson Woodruff Richards** (1895–1973) developed a heart catheterization method. The technique used a hollow, flexible tube inserted into the body to allow the passage of fluids or to widen a passageway. It could be slipped into the heart to diagnose some conditions. French-American physiologist **Andre Cournand** (1895–1988) and German physician **Werner Forssmann** (1904–1979) used the catheter to measure gas pressures in the lung and pulmonary artery. They improved the methods of diagnosing heart diseases and surgically correcting certain heart defects, including the one responsible for blue babies. Richards shared a 1956 Nobel Prize with Cournand and Forssmann for their work.

U.S. surgeon **Norman Edward Shumway** (b. 1923) is another pioneer in cardiac surgery. He developed valve transplantation in open heart surgery. This major advance allows doctors to simply replace the heart valve rather than try to repair it. Shumway also performed the first adult heart transplant in the U.S. in 1968 (see no. 89).

Arthritis, also called "rheumatism," is a painful condition that usually strikes its victims in old age. It disables more people than any other chronic (ongoing) disorder. "Arthritis" is actually a general term for nearly 100 different diseases that cause either inflammation of connective tissues — particularly in joints — or the deterioration of these tissues. The diseases include gout, lupus, degenerative joint disease, Lyme disease and many others. They are most often caused by the wear and tear of aging but can also be caused by immune-system reactions. Research indicates that the nervous system may be involved. One out of seven Americans has some form of arthritis.

Lewis Sarett

Cortisone is a hormone (see no. 52) with many important functions, including the break down of carbohydrates. It is created from cholesterol in the outer layer of the adrenal gland. If the adrenal gland fails to make cortisone, as in Addison's disease, the patient will die.

During World War II, scientists were very interested in cortisone. It was believed that cortisone helped relieve battle fatigue and stress; however, it could not be produced in large quantities. It was not until the war was nearly over, in 1944, that American chemist **Lewis Sarett** used cattle bile, a digestive fluid produced by the liver, to synthesize the hormone. While the new process was too late to help in the war effort, American biochemist **Philip Showalter Hench** (1896–1965) and his colleague **Edward Calvin Kendall** (1886–1972) soon began to investigate the possible medical uses for cortisone.

On September 21, 1948, Hench administered a dose of cortisone to a 20-year-old woman who was completely disabled by arthritis. Only four days later, she was again active and was able to move without pain. Hench then treated 13 other arthritic patients. The results were dramatic. By 1949, he and Kendall were showing their colleagues motion pictures of formerly bedridden patients who were able to run again after treatments of synthetic cortisone. For their amazing work, Hench and Kendall shared a Nobel Prize with the chemist Tadeus Reichstein in 1950.

While cortisone was at first hailed as another "miracle cure," it was soon discovered that while the hormone relieves the pain of arthritis, it does not cure or even slow the progress of the disease. Also, the side effects become significant with long-term use. Some patients develop a kind of diabetes or high blood pressure, so the medications have to be carefully monitored. Still, the hormone's ability to reduce inflamation makes it useful in treating asthma and other allergic reactions, lupus, Hodgkin's disease (a form of cancer), and various skin diseases as well as arthritis. Cortisone and hydrocortisone are also helpful in relieving the itching and inflammation of insect bites and skin conditions such as eczema and psoriasis.

Cortisone was also useful when doctors began performing organ transplants (see nos. 74 and 89). It was found that cortisone helps reduce the body's immune reaction. This otherwise harmful effect can be used to prevent rejection of the donor organ.

73. Tranquilizers
1949

By the 1940s, the methods of Sigmund Freud and his colleagues had become accepted into mainstream medical practices as ways to relieve depression and anxiety (see no. 42). However, psychoanalysis does not work for some serious problems. For example, patients suffering from a condition called manic depression, or bipolar disorder, are usually not helped by conventional psychotherapy. Manic depressive patients are alternately severely depressed and then wildly happy and excitable, making irrational decisions based on their extreme, fleeting moods.

Australian researcher **John Cade** (1912–1980) wondered if some cases of psychosis, particularly manic depression, could be caused by a chemical imbalance in the body. He began testing the urine of psychotic patients and found that lithium, a metallic element, was present there. He then found that lithium had a calming effect on excitable guinea pigs. He tested the substance as a tranqulizer on himself and then on manic depressive patients, and he found that the lithium could normalize their symptoms in five to ten days. However, he also found that lithium is very toxic and that it is very easy to overdose the patient. The levels of lithium in the blood must be carefully monitored. Cade published his revolutionary findings in 1949. For the first time, therapists were able to successfully treat patients suffering from manic depression.

Meanwhile, French researchers were also looking for a way to help psychotic patients. They were trying to find a drug that would slow the metabolism and heart rate. In 1950, chlorpromazine (which is sold under the brand name of **Thorazine**) was developed. It was the first medication to be widely applied to mental disorders and is still the standard drug for people who suffer from such mental illnesses as schizophrenia (skitzoh-FREN-ee-uh). Thorazine was introduced into mental-health institutions in the United States in 1956.

The number of institutionalized mentally ill patients in the U.S. had been steadily increasing, but after the introduction of Thorazine, it began to decrease, from 560,000 institutionalized patients in 1956 to less than 200,000 in 1979. While Thorazine may have been a major factor in the reduced number of hospitalized patients, other factors played a part, too. During the 1960s, U.S. society underwent a number of social changes which included a reevaluation of the methods used to treat psychiatric patients. It was found that in many cases, long-term hospitalization was unnecessary or was deemed too expensive. In addition, a number of different types of outpatient treatments evolved.

With Thorazine and the many other medications that have been developed since the 1950s, doctors now have a variety of methods to deal with mental illnesses. Drugs such as Prozac — introduced in 1987 — and Anaframil, combined with psychotherapy, are promising alternatives in treating depression and manic depression. Today, because of these drugs, many patients who suffer mental disorders are able to lead normal lives.

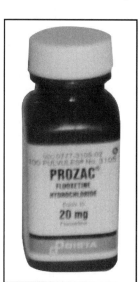

A Bottle of Prozac

74. Kidney Transplants
1950

In 1902, French surgeon **Alexis Carrel** developed the method of joining blood vessels that made organ transplants possible (see no. 49). However, in order for the transplants to be successful, researchers had to find a way to stop the patient's body from rejecting the donor organ. Unfortunately, organs from donors who were not identical twins were usually rejected within a few days or weeks. **Peter Brian Medawar** (see no. 35) and his colleagues discovered in the early 1940s that the rejection of tissue grafts was caused by a reaction of the body's immune system against foreign tissues. Research then focused on stopping the rejection process.

Researchers found that the aggressiveness of the immune system's response depended on how closely related the donor and the patient were. Medawar found that the tissue types were identified on white blood cells (see no. 40) in a similar way that the red-blood-cell groups are identified (see no. 50). Once it was understood that the body tissue types had to be the same, organ transplants became safer.

Organ transplants began with the kidney. In 1950, **Richard H. Lawler** performed the first human kidney transplant in Chicago. Although the transplant itself failed, the patient lived for another four years and died of unrelated causes. Lawler's work broke new ground in transplantation methods. In the mid-1950s, researchers at the Peter Bent Brigham Hospital in Boston found that dogs could survive in good health despite having only one kidney. The other kidney was transplanted to another part of the body to test organ transplant techniques. It required skillful surgery, but since the organ remained in the same individual, there was no chance of rejection. This indicated that a dying patient who had an identical twin might be a suitable patient for a kidney transplant. Since identical twins come from a single egg, they are genetically alike and there would be no danger of organ rejection.

Richard H. Lawler

In 1954, surgeons at the Peter Bent Brigham Hospital in Boston led by **Joseph Murray** (b. 1919) performed the first successful kidney transplant between twins. The patient survived another seven years. Further research found that, when donors came from the same family, about 70 percent of transplants were functioning after one year and 50 percent after five years. Transplants from unrelated donors don't do as well, even with sophisticated modern methods for matching tissue types.

Kidney transplants have been the most successful organ transplant, since patients with kidney failure can be kept healthy by kidney dialysis (see no. 69) while awaiting the transplant. In addition, since a human can live with only one kidney, family members sometimes donate a kidney to save the patient's life. However, organ transplantation is still limited because of a lack of donors. In 1990 more than 19,000 people were on waiting lists for organ transplants, while only 15,160 operations were performed that year.

75. The Structure of DNA
1953

James Watson

The science of genetics arose in 1900 with the rediscovery of **Gregor Mendel**'s work (see no. 32). Geneticists study such things as the unit of inheritance, the gene; the various forms of genes that govern a trait; the pattern of genes within a chromosome (see no. 53); and the complete set of genes — the genome — that is characteristic of each species.

In 1944, American physician and bacteriologist **Oswald Avery** (1877–1955), Canadian biochemist **Colin MacLeod** (b. 1909) and American bacteriologist **Maclyn McCarty** (b. 1911) proved that deoxyiribonucleic acid (DNA) is the blueprint of heredity. However, until 1953, researchers didn't have a model of how the genetic characteristics are carried from from parent to child.

Rosalind Franklin (1920–1958), a British biophysicist at King's College, London, was using x-rays (see no. 43) when she took clear pictures of pure DNA in London. Shortly afterward, U.S. genetic researcher **James Watson** (b. 1928) and English geneticist **Francis Crick** (b. 1916) of Cambridge University wrote in *Nature* magazine, "This structure has novel features that are of considerable biological interest." In the May 30 issue, they demonstrated that chromosomes consist of long strands of DNA. By using one of Franklin's x-ray pictures, they constructed a molecular model of DNA with its "double helix" structure, which looks something like a spiral staircase. Crick, Watson and **Maurice Wilkins** shared a 1962 Nobel Prize for their work on DNA.

Their model of DNA had a huge impact on biology. With this new way of thinking of how DNA is constructed, research in genetics and biochemistry was revitalized. Later, at the California Institute of Technology and Harvard University, Watson determined how proteins are synthesized in the cells. This opened new possibilities for preventing inherited disorders such as Downs Syndrome, Huntington's disease, and some forms of cancer (see no. 34).

Although the shape of DNA had been determined, however, it was still very difficult to find locate the specific genes that control traits. In 1990, **J. Craig Venter**, a researcher at the National Institutes of Health, developed a technique called "expressed sequence tagging" to use in finding human genes. The method targets only the DNA sequences that are used in a cell, allowing biologists to find specific genes quickly. Venter used this method to determine the location of several thousand human genes, more than doubling the number previously known.

Venter's new technique is used by the **Human Genome Project**, which began in 1990. The project is an international effort to map the approximately 100,000 genes on the 23 human chromosomes and to sequence the three billion pairs of DNA that make up the genes. The goal is to understand genetic diseases like muscular dystrophy. The work is projected to last 15 years.

76. The Heart-Lung Machine
1953

The heart-lung machine is a device that maintains the body's circulation and ensures adequate oxygen content in the blood. It is used during operations like open heart surgery (see no. 71) to bypass the circulatory system of the heart and lungs. It works by drawing blood from the veins, reoxygenating it, and pumping it back into the arteries. While the machine can temporarily bypass the function of the heart and lungs, it is not meant for long-term use.

The heart-lung machine was developed in 1953 by **Dr. John Gibbon** (b. 1903) of the Jefferson Medical College in Philadelphia. He began working on the machine in 1930, after he assisted in an operation on a patient who had a blood clot blocking the artery between her heart and her lungs. The woman died, and because of her death, Gibbon decided that he would invent a machine that could work for the heart and lungs during operations, allowing the surgeons more time to work.

The first machine used a hollow metal cylinder which spun rapidly, using centripetal force to make the blood inside the cylinder move up onto the inner surface of the cylinder. Oxygen was then fanned over the spinning blood so the cells would absorb some of it. The process worked, but it was too slow. Gibbons and his colleagues improved the machine by covering the inside of the cylinder with a wire mesh that agitated the blood, allowing it to absorb oxygen more quickly. The design change worked well. In 1953, Gibbons operated on an 18-year-old woman for 45 minutes; for 29 minutes her heart was stopped, with the new machine taking over the functions of her heart and lungs.

Before this invention, a heart operation could not last more than ten minutes because permanent brain damage would result if blood circulation were stopped for any longer. In modern times, major surgery can sometime last for several hours, especially in organ transplants (see nos. 74 and 89) and reconstructive surgeries. The pumps used today in the "heart" part of the modern heart-lung machines are roller pumps, which pump the blood smoothly and gently, minimizing the damage to the red blood cells. The "lung" part of the machine, called an "oxygenator," supplies oxygen to the blood and removes carbon dioxide. In addition to reoxygenating the blood, the machine can also be used to cool the blood during surgery, decreasing the patient's body temperature. This slows the metabolism and prevents stress on the major organs.

**Dr. John Gibbon With His
Heart-Lung Machine**

83

Polio Vaccine
1953

Poliomyelitis, commonly known as polio, is a severe infection caused by one of the three types of virus in the genus *Enterovirus*. It is spread by contact with a polio patient or with the feces of an infected person. Young children are most susceptible, but older people can also be stricken. The most famous of these was U.S. President Franklin D. Roosevelt, who contracted the disease in 1921, at the age of 39. Although Roosevelt survived the disease, he lost the use of his legs.

The virus enters the body through the mouth and invades the bloodstream. Mild cases of polio show no symptoms or just a few symptoms, such as a headache, sore throat, and slight fever. In these cases, patients completely recover in one to three days.

If the virus enters the central nervous system, however, it will attack the motor neurons and can cause lesions on the nerves that result in paralysis. The arms and legs are most often affected. About half of polio patients fully recover from cases in which the nervous system is invaded. The remaining patients suffer from mild disabilities. Those who develop serious cases of polio may become permanently disabled, requiring the use of the iron lung (see no. 65) if paralysis affects the muscles used for breathing.

Polio epidemics were once common among school-age children. The early treatment for paralyzed victims was to immobilize the limbs in casts and splints. However, the Australian nurse **Elizabeth Kenny** (1886–1952) developed a method of active physical therapy to treat paralyzed polio victims. She began stimulating and reeducating the paralyzed muscles of her patients, with great success.

In the early 1950s, there were up to 50,000 cases of polio in the U.S. each year. By 1951, all three strains of the polio virus had been identified. American microbiologist **Jonas Edward Salk** (1914–1995) began to work on a vaccine that would immunize against all three viruses. He and his associates developed an injected vaccine containing dead polio virus. The first tests of the vaccine included Salk's own three children. After field tests of up to 700,000 children in 1953 and 1954, the vaccine became widely available. By May 1955, more than four million children in the U.S. had been vaccinated against polio.

While the good news of Salk's vaccine was hailed by ringing church bells and sounding factory sirens, he knew that it was not entirely effective against one strain of the virus. Research continued. In 1960, after extensive testing, an oral live-virus vaccine was introduced by Polish-American micro-biologist **Albert Bruce Sabin** (see no. 83). The average annual incidence of polio dropped from 37,864 in the period between 1955 and 1956 to just 570 between 1961 and 1965.

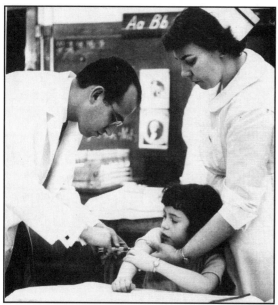

Dr. Jonas Salk Giving Vaccine

78. The Birth Control Pill
1955

Before reliable contraceptives were invented, there was little an adult woman could do to avoid getting pregnant if she was sexually active. Modern contraceptive methods allow couples to determine when to have children and to control the size of their families. The birth control pill is one of the easiest and most reliable contraceptives to use.

Birth control through manipulation of the body's hormones was impossible until American chemist **Percy Lavon Julian** (1899–1975) found that a byproduct of soybean oil could be transformed into an equivalent of the female sex hormone progesterone (proh-JESS-tuhr-ohn). This hormone regulates ovulation, the release of eggs from a woman's ovaries. Then **Russell Marker** in the 1940s discovered that an extract from the yam could easily be made into progesterone, too. A sample of the extract was sent to American biologist **Gregory Pincus** (1903–1967). In 1955, Pincus found that if progesterone was taken in pill form, the chemical prevented ovulation. While Pincus was not really interested in developing a new form of birth control, birth control advocate **Margaret Sanger** (1883–1966) seized upon the discovery and began to make plans.

Sanger found funding for Pincus to research the process of hormonal birth control, and clinical trials were held in Boston and in Puerto Rico. By 1957, "the Pill" had been approved for use in the U.S. Taken once a day, it soon became the most popular birth control method among American women. Along with such modern contraceptives came a change in social attitudes regarding sex in the 1960s. One result was that there was a significant increase in the incidence of sexually transmitted diseases in the decades that followed. With new fears brought about by the AIDS epidemic during the 1990s (see no.

Gregory Pincus

96), however, abstinence again became a common practice for both men and women.

In 1991 the FDA approved the use of Norplant, a contraceptive that is implanted under the skin on the inside of a woman's upper arm. The implant consists of six matchstick-size flexible tubes that contain a synthetic version of progesterone, called progestin. Released slowly and steadily over a five-year period, the drug inhibits ovulation and thickens cervical mucus, preventing sperm from traveling into the uterus. Meanwhile, a new use for birth control pills, as a post-coital (or "morning after") method of preventing pregnancy, was approved by the FDA in 1997.

While hormonal birth control methods have changed women's lives, they also have some serious side effects such as nausea, weight gain, and an increased tendency toward blood clots. However, they may also decrease the risk of cancer of the ovaries, breast cysts, and premenstrual syndrome (PMS). As with any prescribed medication, women should consult with their doctors before making the decision to use the pill.

Ultrasonics is the study of all sound-like waves with a frequency above the range of normal human hearing. Both the waves and the vibrations that produce them are called **ultrasound**. Ultrasound is generated by sending an alternating electrical current across the opposite faces of a plate, causing the plate to vibrate, which creates a "resonance," an amplification of the sound. Discovered by **Paul Jacques** and **Pierre Curie** (see no. 43) in the 1880s, ultrasound was an interesting novelty. However, by 1930 it had become a small branch of physics research.

Like normal sound waves, ultrasound waves move through water and through solid materials much more rapidly than through air. Therefore, they are useful for getting a picture of objects that are under large bodies of water (as with sonar) or within a solid body. It was in 1957 that Scottish doctor **Ian Donald** began using ultrasound for medical diagnosis.

To obtain an ultrasound image, a wandlike "transducer" is glided across a specific area of the body upon a film of liquid or gel. The liquid prevents air from getting in the way and interfering with the ultrasound waves. When the waves contact denser structures within the body, part of the sound energy is reflected back to the body surface, where it is read electronically and converted into a picture. The technique causes the skin to become slightly warm, but there are no known side effects.

Donald started by using ultrasound to locate tumors. Later, he began using it to examine babies in the womb. This technique continues to be used in pregnancy to determine if there is more than one baby, as well as each baby's position, its sex, and its age. It is also useful for evaluating fetal movements, such as breathing, heartbeat, and mouth and hand movements that can indicate the future development of important early behaviors such as suckling and grasping. Donald was at first concerned that ultrasound, like the x-ray (see no. 43), might cause problems such as cancer. Fortunately, ultrasound is safe for both mother and child.

Donald's work with ultrasound led to other diagnostic uses in medicine. It can be used to provide information about tumors and cysts that cannot be obtained by normal x-ray studies. Other uses for ultrasound are the echocardiogram, for examining patients with inherited or acquired heart conditions, and a Doppler ultrasound technique that can detect the blood flow in the veins and arteries.

Ultrasound is also used in dentistry and in surgery. For example, strong pulses of ultrasound can be sent into the body to shatter kidney stones and gallstones in a process called "lithotripsy." Ultrasound is also used in physical therapy, massage and chiropractic work to heat and relax the muscles and joints.

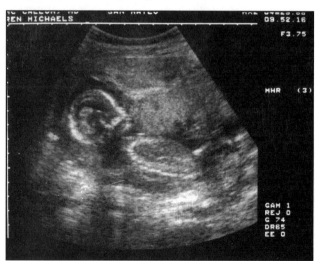

An Ultrasound of a Human Fetus

80. The Artificial Pacemaker
1958

The heart's beating is controlled by the pacemaker, which is a knot of tissue in the heart muscle. The pacemaker starts the wave of muscle contraction known as the heartbeat. Heart disease that involves the pacemaker cells can cause rapid, slow, or irregular heartbeats, or the heartbeat may stop altogether. An artificial pacemaker can stimulate or regulate the heartbeat, thus saving the patient's life.

In the late 1940s, researcher **Paul M. Zoll** was studying coronary heart disease at Harvard University. He was frustrated by the death of a "very nice lady," 60 years old, who died of a diseased pacemaker, Zoll said, "when nothing else was wrong with her."

Zoll found part of the solution at a meeting of the Boston Surgical Society in 1950. Two Canadian surgeons gave a presentation on their experiments in lowering body temperature while performing open heart surgery on dogs. The dogs' hearts frequently slowed or stopped beating during the surgery, and the researchers described how they had passed a wire electrode down to the heart to stimulate the pacemaker and restore the heartbeat.

On his return to Harvard, Zoll also began experimenting with the electric stimulator on dogs. Zoll modified the device to better suit his purpose, and by 1952 he was ready for his first human experiment. His mechanism placed the electrodes on the outside of the body, one on each side of the chest. His first patient had to be so close to death that the risk of electrocution was outweighed by the threat of death. It happened that the father of one of Zoll's neighbors had been rushed to the emergency room. Zoll managed to "pace" him, that is, restore his heartbeat electronically, for 20 minutes before he died. A month later, Zoll paced another patient for 48 hours. This patient was gradually weaned from the artificial pacemaker and sent home. He lived for six months before dying of a heart attack.

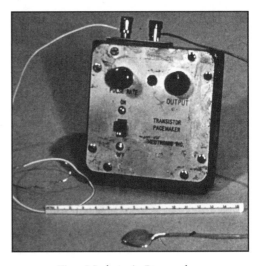

First Medtronic Pacemaker

Following these successes, Zoll had a manufacturing company build the prototype of a cardiac monitor, a machine to monitor the patient's heartbeat. This made it possible for the pacemaker to be automatically turned on when the patient's heart rate dropped too low. However, Zoll found that the long-term users had a continuing problem with chest pains and skin burns. This led to the invention of an internal artificial pacemaker.

Invented in 1958 by American biomedical engineer **Wilson Greatbatch** (b. 1919), in cooperation with doctors **William M. Chardack** and **Andrew A. Gage**, the first internal model was a small, flat, plastic disk powered by a tiny battery. It was implanted in the body and connected by wires sewn directly onto the heart. The wires emitted rhythmic electric impulses that triggered the heart's action.

New pacemakers use wires implanted in the heart through veins. They can be controlled by an external magnetic switch or can be preset for the patient's individual needs. Future pacemakers may react to changes in body temperature and increases in the need for oxygen.

The practice of preventive medicine has become highly valued in modern times. In the 1800s, both scientists and politicians became aware of the medical importance of good personal hygiene and of public health practices (see nos. 19 and 22). It was not until the 20th century, however, that the practice of preventive medicine became commonplace.

The focus at first was upon larger issues, such as vaccinations and clean air and water, rather than on personal lifestyle choices. However, scientists began to notice that such things as diet, smoking, and excercise have a great influence on the health of a population.

In particular, there was a rapid decline in breastfeeding during the 1950s and early 1960s, after artificial formulas became readily available, was noted with alarm. By 1971, breastfeeding had reached its lowest popularity. The decline in breastfeeding was accompanied by a slightly higher infant death rate. This attracted the attention of scientists, who began to study the effects of breastfeeding on the health of both mothers and babies. Their studies found that mother's milk has great nutritional value and also contains antibodies that help the baby fight off disease. Breastfed babies grow more quickly, are healthier, have a lower death rate, and may even have higher IQs. In recognition of this, some states, such as California, have passed legislation to permit mothers to breastfeed in public places.

Smoking is another important factor in individual health choices. In 1958, U.S. epidemiologists

Edward Cuyler Hammond (1912–1986) and **Daniel Horn** published the startling results of a two-year study of men who smoke cigarettes. They found that more of these men died than was typical of nonsmokers. The causes of death were mainly heart disease, lung cancer, and other forms of cancer including cancer of the esophagus and larynx. The dramatic evidence that smoking is hazardous to health convinced many people to give up smoking — including Dr. Horn himself! Since this report and many others with similar findings were published, public opinion has forced a ban on cigarette advertising on television and has brought laws preventing second-hand smoke in public places.

Diet has also become a large issue in preventive medicine. Research has found that diets high in fat and cholesterol are directly linked to a higher incidence of heart disease and strokes. Obesity is also linked to a high-fat diet, putting people at risk for cardiovascular problems, diabetes, and other disorders. In contrast, low fat diets that are high in fiber are believed to help prevent breast and colon cancer, lower blood pressure, and help to maintain a healthy weight. Certain foods, such as broccoli and carrots, also protect the body against cancer. Dentistry has also reduced tooth and gum disease by promoting brushing, flossing and regular checkups.

The concept that health can be improved by vaccinations, proper diet, exercise, regular health examinations and good personal habits has now become prevalent.

SMOKING IS VERY GLAMOROUS

AMERICAN CANCER SOCIETY

Anti-Smoking Ad

82. Cardiopulmonary Resuscitation
1958

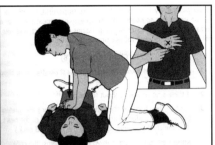

Cardiopulmonary resuscitation (kar-dee-oh-PUL-mon-airy ruh-sus-i-TAE-shen), commonly known as CPR, is a first-aid technique that provides blood circulation to a person whose heart has stopped. After four to six minutes without the flow of blood,

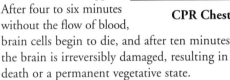

CPR Chest Compression

brain cells begin to die, and after ten minutes the brain is irreversibly damaged, resulting in death or a permanent vegetative state.

One part of the technique was developed in 1732 by the Scottish surgeon **William Tossach**, who revived an unconcious coal miner through mouth-to-mouth resusitation. Centuries later, **Dr. Edward Schafer** developed a method of chest pressure to stimulate respiration. His method was adoped by the American Red Cross in 1910 and was taught for many years.

In 1926, officials at a power company became concerned about the number of workers who had been killed by accidental electrocution, which among other things interfered with the function of the heart. There was no method for reviving them. They decided to have some specialists at **Johns Hopkins Medical School** work on the problem.

The team was made up of a neurologist, **O.R. Langworthy**; a physiologist, **R.D. Hooker**; and an electrical engineer, **William B. Kouwenhoven**. They had little success until 1930, when their attention was drawn to a new study. It was reported that a fatal irregularity of the heartbeat was reversed in a dog's heart, which was exposed by surgery, through electrical stimulation. Upon investigating, the team found that this was true, but both this method and massaging the heart by hand required major surgery to expose the heart.

Kouwenhoven, however, noticed that when they applied electricity to the heart, the chest leaped as though it had been thumped. He began to consider whether the heart could be restarted by applying a regular and rhythmic pressure to the chest. His first attempt, on a cat, was a success. He began testing the method on other animals and then at on patients at the hospital.

In 1958, a two-year-old child's heart stopped beating. **Henry Bahnson** knew of Kouwenhoven's method and used it on the child, saving his life. From then on, CPR became necessary training for all doctors, ambulance drivers, firefighters and other first-aid workers. The American Red Cross endorsed CPR in 1963.

To perform CPR, the victim is placed lying down, face up, and his airway is opened (by tilting the head slightly back, dropping the chin, and freeing the throat of obstructions). If the victim is not breathing, mouth-to-mouth resuscitation is performed. If no pulse is found, the rescuer should quickly summon medical help and then begin CPR. First he places the heel of his hand against the lower third of the victim's breastbone, and begins to pump downward — firmly, but without harming the victim — counting 15 pumps in 10 to 12 seconds. After a minute of CPR alternating with mouth-to-mouth resuscitation, the pulse is checked. CPR should continue until the victim's pulse returns and the victim resumes breathing, or until medical help arrives.

CPR has saved thousands of lives by maintaining oxygenated blood flow in patients, particularly heart attack and drowning victims, until they reach the emergency room.

83. **Oral Vaccinations**
1961

While the polio vaccine introduced by **Jonas Salk** in 1954 was hailed as a "miracle cure" by thankful parents (see no. 77), Salk knew that it was not completely effective against one of the three strains of polio. The other flaw was that sometimes the vaccine provided immunity for only a short period of time. Some children had to be revaccinated on a regular schedule to remain safe from polio.

After Salk's vaccine was introduced, Polish-American microbiologist **Albert Bruce Sabin** (1906–1993) began seeking a better polio vaccine. A talented researcher, Sabin dedicated his life to developing vaccines. He knew that Salk's vaccine was created using dead virus material, so he began developing a live-virus vaccine.

By using a live virus, which would cause the body to produce a higher number of antibodies against the disease, Sabin was hoping to give children permanent immunity against the ravages of polio. After successful field tests

Albert Sabin

in Mexico, Europe, and Russia between 1957 and 1959, the Sabin live-virus vaccine was introduced in the U.S. in 1961, replacing the earlier dead-virus vaccine. An added advantage to the new vaccine was that it was an **oral vaccine**, which avoided the need for shots. However, it still had to be given in several doses, the first three each one month apart, with boosters at about age five and any time there was an outbreak of the disease.

While the vaccines were a huge success, there were also a few failures. In very rare cases the vaccine itself caused cases of polio.

In 1985 the World Health Organization began distributing the oral polio vaccine in a program to eradicate polio worldwide by the year 2000. The last reported case of polio in the western hemisphere was in 1991.

Although vaccines have been developed for many other common diseases, such as cholera, anthrax, and rabies (see no. 38), most of them are injected, rather than taken orally. However, there is a great need for the development of oral vaccines, which are easier to distribute and to take, for the most common diseases, such as influenza. In June 1997, the British drug company Cortecs announced they were conducting clinical trials on an oral flu vaccine and that the trials were showing good results. Flu is not dangerous in most cases, but it can sometimes be fatal for people who are very young, elderly, have vulnerable immune systems (such as AIDS patients; see no. 96) or are prone to respiratory problems like asthma. Since new strains of flu are evolving all the time, people who get flu vaccines need to get a new inoculation every year. Sometimes there are several virulent flu strains circulating during the same period, making several shots neccessary.

Laser Surgery
1964

The **laser** produces a beam of light that is very useful because it is "coherent" light, made up of light waves of a single frequency all moving along together in unison. This light beam is produced by a process known as stimulated emission. The word "laser" is an acronym for "light amplification by stimulated emission of radiation." Laser beams are very powerful and can be used to cut, burn, or measure distances and for many other purposes.

The fundamental principles of the laser were established long before it was built. The famous physicist **Albert Einstein** (1879–1955) theorized the possibility of stimulated emission, in 1916. The possible existence of high-energy photons (light particles) was discussed by **V.A. Fabrikant** in 1940. These two fundamental ideas were followed by 20 years of developing technology for using coherent light.

In July 1960, the American physicist **Theodore Harold Maiman** (b. 1927) first demonstrated the successful operation of a laser at Hughes Research Laboratories. He used a ruby crystal to generate a pulse of coherent red light. Only four years later, the laser was used for the first time in medicine. **H. Vernon Ingram** saw that the laser could be used in eye surgery to avoid the need for any incisions. One particularly successful eye operation using lasers has been the reattachment of a detached retina. In this situation, the retina has developed a small hole, allowing fluid from inside the eye to seep out and causing the retina to lift off the back of the eye. If the hole is not repaired, the patient will go blind. An eye surgeon can apply a single pulse of the laser beam — only .001 seconds long — to the hole, causing a burn that results in a tiny scar that closes the hole. The

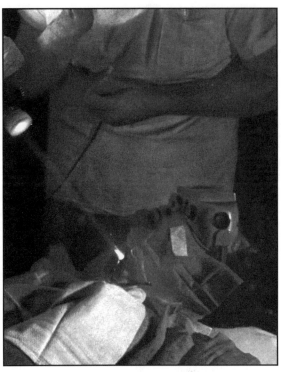

A Man Undergoing Laser Sugery on his Neck

first laser surgery inspired researchers to look at the possibilities of lasers in medicine in a new way.

By 1967, a laser had been developed that could cut and seal blood vessels at the same time. Lasers can be used to seal tiny blood vessels in the skin without damaging deeper tissues. Doctors can now painlessly vaporize a surface tumor or cut into an organ while cauterizing the blood vessels. Another important use of the laser is in cauterizing stomach ulcers using an endoscope (see no. 86). Lasers can also be used to clear cholesterol blockages in arteries. Some dermatolotical procedures can now be done in a doctor's office — with no bleeding, little or no pain, and less scarring — by using a laser.

Beta Blockers
1964

Sir James Black

Beta blockers are drugs that block a muscle's beta receptors, which are cells in the muscle tissue that react to various hormones. For example, if these receptors are blocked in the heart, the heart muscle doesn't react as strongly when stimulated by the hormone adrenaline (see no. 52). Beta receptors are concentrated mainly in the heart, lungs, kidneys and blood vessels, which makes these organs particularly sensitive to hormones like adrenaline.

It was known by 1948 that some muscles have two kinds of receptors, alpha and beta. British pharmacologist **Sir James Whyte Black** (b. 1924) then theorized that there might be a way to block the beta receptors, preventing the organs from reacting to hormones. He began working on this theory in the 1960s. His first successful beta blocker was propanolol, which was developed in 1964. Propanol was soon being used to treat heart conditions like angina (constriction of the heart muscle due to lack of blood supply) and arrhythmia (irregular heartbeat) (see no. 80), as well as other problems like high blood pressure and migraine headaches. Beta blockers can even be used to treat milder problems such as stage fright and glaucoma.

Drug manufacturers hailed beta blockers as the new "wonder drugs." They advertised the products by showing athletes in action, promoting the fact that the beta blockers did not adversely affect their abilities. In fact, the beta blockers actually seemed to improve performance. Unfortunately, by 1974 the side effects began to appear. Some patients had heart failure. Others' asthma attacks increased in intensity. More research produced other beta blockers that did not have the same adverse side effects, although some side effects do remain. These include weakness and drowsiness (which disappear after the medication is discontinued), and sometimes wheezing. People with asthma, bronchitis or emphysema should use beta blockers under the close supervision of their doctors.

In the meantime, Black had continued his own research on beta blockers, and in 1972 he had discovered cimetidine. This new beta blocker blocked the receptors in the digestive system, helping to prevent peptic ulcers. Cimetidine is now also used in patients suffering from cirrhosis, a common cause of death in the U.S., by controlling stomach and intestinal bleeding. Cirrhosis is a degenerative liver disease often caused by hepatitis, toxic drugs, or chronic alcoholism. Black recieved a Nobel Prize in 1988.

86. The Endoscope
1965

The term "**endoscope**" describes any instrument used to look inside the body. The most commonly used type of endoscope is a lighted tube that is attached to a viewing device and inserted through the mouth or other opening into the body. The cystoscope, one type of endoscope, was first invented by German doctor **Max Nitze** (1848–1906) in 1877, but because his original model used a rigid tube, its uses were limited. In the 1950s, however, a flexible tube was used so the endoscope could bend and twist through the body. With this new flexibility, the instrument was used more often in other places, such as the intestines.

In 1965, British inventor **Harold Hopkins** (d. 1995) improved the endoscope's lenses, allowing the doctor a clearer view. Doctors were then able to use the instrument to detect ulcers, tumors and lesions. In many cases, major exploratory surgery was no longer necessary to diagnose these conditions. With a small cut or insertion through a natural opening, the doctor could look directly at the suspect tissues.

With the modern inventions of laser surgery (see no. 84) and fiber optics, doctors could also perform biopsies (removing a small tissue sample for examination), burn off growths, and seal blood vessels, again avoiding major surgery and lengthy hospital stays. Removing polyps in the lower intestine using an endoscope is a major method of preventing colon cancer.

There are a number of different types of endoscopes used today. Some use tiny cameras to view the interior of the body on a television screen. Others have tiny microchip sensors that feed information to a computer. Common types of endoscopes and their uses are the cystoscope for the bladder (which is still a rigid tube), the bronchoscope for the lungs, the otoscope for the ear, the arthroscope for the knee and other joints, and the laparascope for general abdominal procedures as well as the female reproductive system.

The most common surgery performed through endoscopy is the biopsy of suspected cancers. The endoscope has become an essential part of modern medicine, and many thousands of endoscopic procedures are conducted in the U.S. every year.

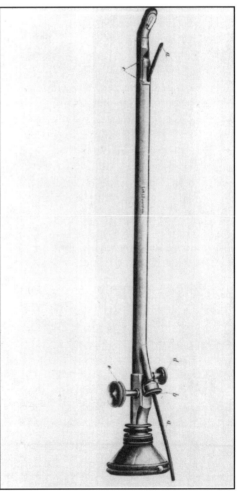

Nitze's Cystoscope; 1877

Artificial Blood
1966

As **William Harvey** found in 1628, blood is the essential substance in the body. With the development of blood transfusions and the understanding of blood types (see nos. 18 and 50), it became possible to save patients who once would have bled to death. Transfusions also became a valuable technique in some medical procedures in which the doctor would deliberately remove some of the blood and then replace it after treatment, as with kidney dialysis (see no. 69).

However, there has always been the problem of a lack of donors for transfusions. Although blood is quickly made in the body and many people donate blood on a regular basis, there are times when there is not enough blood to satisfy the needs of patients.

In 1966, American researchers **Leland C. Clark** (b. 1918) and **F. Gollan** began experimenting with a solution of fluorocarbon and water. They knew that fluorocarbon absorbs oxygen from the air, as blood does. When they dropped some mice into the liquid and held them under the surface, the mice did not drown. As the liquid filled their lungs, the fluorocarbon had combined with the oxygen in the water and passed into their blood.

By the following year, researcher Henry Sloviter was transfusing rabbits with a liquid solution containing fluorocarbon. As long as he did not replace more than one third of the rabbits' blood, the experiments were successful. However, researchers were still a long way from experimenting on humans.

It was not until 1979 that the first human received artificial blood. Japanese researcher **Ryochi Naito** injected himself with nearly half a pint (200 ml) of the liquid. While he survived his experiments, even more research was needed before the substance could be given to a patient. However, in the 1980s, with the advent of the AIDS epidemic (see no. 96), development of artificial blood became even more urgent. Normal human blood from donors must be refrigerated and can be contaminated by diseases like AIDS and hepatitis.

Today, artificial blood contains a substance that mimics hemoglobin, the molecule in the blood that carries oxygen through the body. While there is still no true substitute for blood, artificial blood is sometimes used to supplement human blood in transfusions when patients often need large amounts of blood because of severe burns or other emergency situations. The artificial blood, while supplying the body's oxygen needs, doesn't carry the other essential ingredients of blood, like the disease-fighting white blood cells (see no. 40). In addition, not all patients' blood types are compatible with the artificial blood. Researchers hope to find answers to these problems and to develop an artificial blood that will be tolerated by people of all blood types.

Real Blood Plasma Packs

The **CAT scan**, or computerized axial tomography scan, is a high-tech system used to x-ray the interior of the body. The CAT scan is very accurate for finding and establishing the size of brain tumors, blood clots and other brain damage, as well as finding the location, type and size of injuries or diseases of the central nervous system, lungs, abdomen and pelvis.

In medical terms, "tomography" is a method for obtaining views of a particular section of the body, eliminating the x-ray shadows that the bones and organs throw in front of and behind that section. "Axial" suggests the series of cross-sectional x-ray images that is taken in the CAT scan, and "computerized" refers to the way the images are then combined by a computer into a single, two-dimensional picture. During a CAT scan, the patient lies on a table. The x-ray emitter is rotated around the body section that is to be examined. Electronic sensors pick up the rays emerging from the CAT scanner and feed them into a computer, combining them into a 3-D image. This image is then displayed on a television screen and photographed, and it can be stored on a computer disk for further reference.

British electrical engineer **Godfrey Hounsfield** (b. 1919) began developing the CAT scanner in the late 1960s. In the meantime, South African–American physicist **Allan Cormack** (b. 1924) was working independently on the same idea. Cormack's main work was theoretical research on subatomic particle interactions. He determined how strong the x-rays need to be to produce CAT scan images. The first model of the CAT scanner was developed in 1967, and the first commercial CAT scanner was successfully introduced in 1972. It was quickly brought into common use at most major medical centers. Hounsfield and Cormack shared a Nobel Prize in 1979 for the invention of the CAT scan.

Godfrey Hounsfield

The CAT scan has revolutionized the diagnosis of injuries and diseases. For example, in serious head-injury cases, CAT scans can find bleeding inside the skull, which causes damage because of the excessive pressure on the delicate tissues of the brain. Previously, identifying this problem would have required brain surgery. CAT scans are often used in planning therapy for cancer, since the size and extent of tumors can be determined without major surgery. In addition, CAT scans are useful in plastic surgery (see no. 68). The surgeon can use the three-dimensional images in planning reconstructive as well as cosmetic surgery. With modern computer methods, the patient can be shown a computerized picture of how he or she will look after the surgery.

With the first kidney transplant performed in 1950 (see no. 74) and the first liver transplant in 1963, research into organ transplants intensified. However, kidneys and livers proved to be relatively easy to work with, while some organs are more difficult.

In the case of kidneys, patients can be maintained by dialysis (see no. 69) for long periods of time. The liver, furthermore, is capable of regenerating itself, so just a portion of a liver can be transplanted into a patient — if the transplant is successful, it will then grow to accommodate its new body's needs. The heart, however, is another matter entirely. Without a beating heart, the body can only be maintained for a short period of time on a heart-lung machine. Therefore, **heart transplants** became a major focus of new research.

In 1961, American surgeon Norman Edward Shumway (b. 1923) succeeded in transplanting a heart from one dog to another.

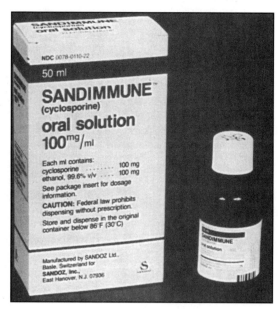

Cyclosporine Medication

The dog survived for three weeks before the new heart was rejected. Only three years later, a patient received a chimpanzee's heart. The new heart was rejected in this case as well.

Then, on December 3, 1967, the world was stunned by the news that South African surgeon **Christiaan Barnard** (b. 1922) had performed the first successful human heart transplant. He had used the heart of a 24-year-old person who had died of head injuries and placed it into 54-year-old Louis Washkansky. Washkansky lived for 18 days, then died of pneumonia.

While Barnard's first transplant was successful, rejection was still a danger to the patient. As with kidney transplants, the patient's tissue type had to match the donor's, or the body would not accept the transplant — and even if the tissue types matched, the body might still reject the new organ. In the early 1970s, anti-rejection drugs called cyclosporines were discovered. These new drugs were not widely available for another ten years, but they would come to change the nature of organ transplants. Cyclosporines supress the body's immune system, preventing rejection of the new organ and dramatically increasing the survival rate of transplant patients despite the serious side effects. With this new ability, transplants have become common.

In modern times, many kinds of transplants are performed, including heart, lung, bone marrow (see no. 91), pancreas and multi-organ transplants. Still, organ transplants are limited by the lack of donors. There is new hope, however, with the possibility of growing new organs from the patient's own tissues (see no. 100).

Microsurgery
1968

Microsurgery uses magnifying systems, computers, lasers and other precision tools to perform surgery at a microscopic level. Using these techniques, surgeons can reattach severed limbs — repairing even tiny blood vessels and nerves — operate on the inner ear, remove tumors of the spinal cord, use microscopes in brain surgery and perform other delicate operations that were once considered impossible.

Microsurgery actually began as early as 1912, when Alexis Carrel invented a method of joining blood vessels together end to end (see no. 49). With this knowledge, researchers began working on better methods of surgery. By the 1960s, better microscopes, fine needles, silk thread, and a greater understanding of the human body allowed surgeons to sew tiny blood vessels together. However, they were still unable to precisely reattach nerves, the essential step in reattaching an arm, leg or finger. If the nerves are not attached properly, the limb may not work correctly and feeling will not return to them. Without the sense of touch, many people would be unable to resume their normal activities.

In 1968, the Japenese research team of **Komatsu and Tamai** used a technique to reconnect nerves that was introduced only a year earlier to reattach a thumb. Their ground-breaking surgery pioneered the science of microsurgery.

An interesting addition to microsurgery is the occasional use of leeches. Leeches were once used to treat many illnesses incorrectly (see no. 8). In some microsurgeries, blood does not flow through the reattached member adequately. Leeches are attached, and they drain the excess blood.

They also secrete a substance that prevents the blood from clotting, which also promotes circulation.

Today, surgeons use microsurgery combined with an arthroscope, a type of endoscope (see no. 86), which can be inserted into a joint through very small incisions. This procedure can be done on an outpatient basis (meaning the patient does not have to stay in the hospital to recover) because it allows for much faster recovery than traditional surgery did. Another use of microsurgery is reversing a vasectomy, the procedure of cutting the sperm-transporting tubes (however not all men regain their fertility after the reversal is done). In addition, microsurgery now also uses lasers (see no. 84) in very precise surgeries, allowing the surgeon to literally vaporize a tiny growth.

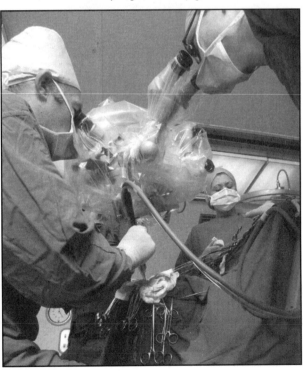

Microsurgery Being Performed

91. Bone Marrow Transplants
1968

Robert A. Good

The **bone marrow transplant** has become an essential line of defense in treating several kinds of cancer (see no. 34), particularly certain types of leukemia and immune deficiency diseases. The actual process of a bone marrow transplant is difficult for the patient, however. Leukemia patients only get bone marrow transplants if they have already endured chemotherapy (see no. 60) and it has failed (chemotherapy is successful 60 percent of the time).

Once a suitable donor has been located, these patients must first have treatments to kill their own bone marrow. Then the donor's bone marrow is injected into the patient. The new bone marrow migrates to the bones, and if the procedure is successful, the marrow will begin to reproduce itself and make more blood. The patient must remain isolated until the doctor is sure that the treatment has been effective, because one of the greatest dangers at this point is infection. Since all of the patient's bone marrow has been destroyed, the patient has no resistance to disease because there are no new white blood cells to fight off foriegn bodies (see no. 40). A simple cold can prove fatal. If the transplant is successful, the new bone marrow will grow and spread, curing the patient.

The first bone marrow transplant to cure immunodeficiency disease was performed in 1968 by **Robert A. Good**. His patient, David Camp, was the 13th male member of his family to be diagnosed with immune deficiency disease. The other 12 had died. Good and his colleagues worried about the potential for tissue rejection. Finally, Good realized that they must use the bone marrow from one of Camp's four sisters. Although it wasn't a perfect match, they used it anyway. The transplant took, but then the transplanted cells began to destroy all of Camp's remaining blood cells. Rather than try to kill the transplanted cells, the doctors performed a second transplant, using more of his sister's marrow. The transplanted cells flourished in his body, and Camp survived.

The bone marrow transplant has improved dramatically since these early attempts. It is now used to treat several types of leukemia, Hodgkin's disease, inherited immune system disorders, plasma cell disorders and severe aplastic anemia, in which the bone marrow lacks some or all of the types of blood cells. Doctors can now separate out the stem cells, the immature cells found in the bone marrow. Research has found that by using only the stem cells, the patient has a better chance of recovery. However, as in every transplant procedure, bone marrow donors are in short supply. Many patients die every year because a suitable donor cannot be found.

The Artificial Heart

The **artificial heart** is still an experimental device, but its development has made great strides since the idea was first introduced. The first known artificial heart was developed by **Alexis Carrel** (see no. 49) and **Charles A. Lindbergh**, the famous American aviator, in 1936. Carrel used the mechanism to keep different tissues and organs alive by circulating blood through them.

The first successful artificial heart was implanted into a dog in 1957. **Willem Kolff** (see no. 71) and American biomedical engineer **Tetsuzu Akutsu** had developed a heart that kept the animal alive for 1.5 hours. Research-ers later developed four-chambered hearts for temporary use in human beings. In 1963, an artificial heart was used for the first time to take over blood circulation during heart surgery by American surgeon **Michael Ellis de Bakey** (b. 1908).

Six years later, in April 1969, American surgeon and educator **Denton A. Cooley** (b. 1920) performed the first successful implant of a temporary artificial heart. A 47-year-old man received a silicone heart, which kept him alive for 65 hours until a human heart was available for transplant.

The first permanent artificial heart was implanted in **Barney Clark** in December 1982. Named for its designer, **Dr. Robert K. Jarvik** (b. 1946), the Jarvik-7 was implanted by **Dr. William C. DeVries** (b. 1943) and a team of surgeons at the University of Utah Medical Center. The Jarvik-7 was a little larger than a normal human heart and consisted of two chambers that replaced the natural heart's left and right ventricles, or lower chambers. It was attached to the heart's atria, or upper chambers. The artificial heart beat 100 times per minute, pumping about two gallons of blood in that time. It was powered by an air compressor attached outside the body.

Clark was suffering from an inoperable and irreversible deterioration of his heart. Too old to qualify for a heart transplant, Clark volunteered to be the first patient to receive the Jarvik-7. Although he suffered from complications after the surgery, Clark lived for 112 days. His death was due to natural organ failure and circulatory collapse, not to his artificial heart, which was still working properly. There were 90 more implants using the Jarvik-7. One patient lived for 620 days, but he suffered terribly. Such patients were hooked up to machines and stayed in hospital beds for the entire time they lived.

In 1990, artificial hearts were banned in the U.S., partly because there was no way to prevent such suffering with their use. Fortunately, there are other ways to treat heart disease. For example, it can often be alleviated by artificial heart valves and pacemakers.

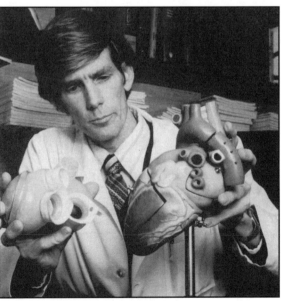

William DeVries

Magnetic Resonance Imaging
1977

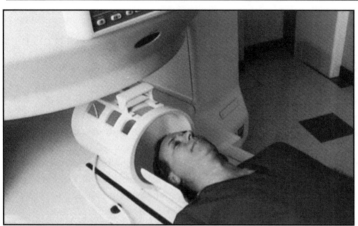

A Man Undergoing an MRI Scan

Magnetic resonance imaging (MRI) is a diagnostic tool used in the field of medicine known as radiology. Radiology is concerned with using certain applications from the study of physics — such as electromagnetic waves, magnetic fields, radioactive compounds and sound waves — to both diagnose and treat diseases. Other tools of radiology include x-rays (see no. 43), radiation therapy (see no. 62), ultrasound (see no. 79) and the CAT scan (see no. 88).

MRI works by placing the patient within a cylinder that contains a strong magnet. The magnet causes all the hydrogen atoms in the fluids and tissues in the body to spin in the same direction. Radio waves are then beamed into the cylinder, changing the alignment of the hydrogen atoms in proportion to the amount of water in the tissue. Thus, the atoms in different kinds of body tissues change their alignment at different rates. Therefore, the computer is able to measure the changes in hydrogen-atom alignment and to translate these signals into a picture that shows all the different tissue densities in the body.

MRI scans are used to check for joint and soft-tissue problems. They are also used to view injuries, tumors, or post-surgical changes in the chest, abdomen, pelvis, brain, and spinal cord. MRI scans don't use radiation, as do x-rays and CAT scans, nor do they use radioactive dyes. Therefore, MRI scans are safer for patients. Another advantage of the MRI is that the doctor can see blood vessels, spinal fluid, cartilage, bone marrow, muscles and ligaments. It can also see through the bones.

MRI is often used to view the area at the back of the brain between the ears, the *posterior fossa,* to detect tumors. It can also help doctors to locate injuries in joints and herniated disks. Patients with pacemakers, artificial heart valves, pins in their joints, or other metal objects implanted in their bodies usually avoid MRI because the powerful magnetic field of the MRI machine may damage or dislodge these objects during the procedure.

American researcher **Raymond V. Damadian** (b. 1936) tested the first MRI scanner on July 2, 1977. His revolutionary new machine allowed doctors to detect cancer and other defects without exposing patients to radiation. This was extremely important to patients who had already been exposed to large amounts of radiation during therapy, and to those patients who had a a form of cancer that was caused by radiation. The Food and Drug Administration (FDA) approved MRI scanners for commercial use in medicine in 1984.

Since the beginning of humanity, conception of a human being required that the ovum travel down the Fallopian tube, meet the sperm, and then implant itself into the womb. However, if a woman's Fallopian tubes were blocked by a deformity or by scar tissue, she could not conceive. This situation has troubled many families who wanted a child.

However, in 1969 gynecologist **Patrick Steptoe** (1913–1988) and physiologist **Robert Edwards**, both from England, surgically removed some eggs from an infertile woman's ovaries, took sperm from her husband, and combined them in a petri dish (hence the term "in vitro," meaning "in the laboratory"). Steptoe left the eggs and sperm together in the petri dish for several days to ensure that fertilization had occurred. Then he implanted the fertilized ovum in the mother's womb. Left to grow naturally, the egg developed into a baby girl. **Louise Brown**, the first "test tube" baby, was born on July 25, 1978, in Lancashire, England. It had taken nearly ten years of experimentation before this first success.

The news produced a storm of media coverage as well as many couples looking for an opportunity to conceive their own children through the new method. The technique has also raised legal, ethical, and religious issues. The Roman Catholic Church, for example, questioned the procedure, asking whether it is appropriate for humans to artificially assist conception.

As research into the technique continued, there have been many advances in the procedure and a greater success rate. For example, if the would-be father is sterile, sperm from a donor or from a sperm bank may be used. If the egg is successfully fertilized, after undergoing several cell divisions, it is usually transferred directly to the mother's — or occasionally a surrogate mother's — body, but sometimes it is frozen for later implantation. One new problem caused by this advanced technology is that there have been several legal battles over custody of frozen embryos after the couples who produced them decided to get a divorce.

Despite the ethical questions that it raises, **in vitro fertilization** is now frequently used to help parents with reproductive problems such as inability to produce eggs, poor sperm quality, or endometriosis (a condition where the inner lining of the uterus grows in abnormal places in the body). Many men and women are now parents thanks to Steptoe's and Edwards' research.

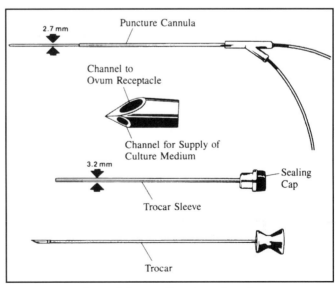

Tools Used for Fertilization of an Ovary

95. Artificial Skin
1981

The skin is the body's largest organ. It regulates body temperature, holds moisture inside, and keeps out bacteria. While skin grafts can be used to cover some injuries, sometimes the damaged area is too large to cover completely with skin from other areas of the patient's body. In the case of severe burns, when the deepest layers of skin have been burned away, it is especially important to cover the damaged areas as soon as possible. Otherwise, the patient can die from dehydration or bacterial infections.

Until the 1960s, patients with burns covering more than 40 percent of their bodies usually died. As medical techniques advanced, the survival rate slowly improved. However, with the development of **artificial skin**, patients with burns covering up to 90 percent of their bodies have begun to survive their terrible injuries.

Artificial skin was invented by **John F. Burke** of Harvard Medical School and by **Ioannis Yannas** (b. 1935) of the Massachusetts Institute of Technology (MIT). It was first used by Yannas in 1981. It is composed of a thin sheet of the mineral silicon, which comprises the outer layer, and an inner layer of collagen, a protein found in cartilage and bone. The inner layer serves as a permanent framework for the skin's regrowth, and the silicon protects the tender new tissues.

Even with modern medical advances, using artificial skin is not an easy process. First the burned tissues must be removed. Sometimes a patch of healthy skin is sent to the laboratory, where a sheet of new skin is grown using new techniques for cloning cells (see no. 99). Meanwhile, a sheet of artificial skin is stitched or stapled over the wound. The deep layers of skin regenerate as the skin cells slowly grow into the collagen framework.

When the patient's skin has replaced enough of the damaged area, the silicone layer is removed, and it is replaced by surface-layer skin from the lab or from split-thickness skin grafts on other parts of the body. Since the deeper layers of skin are already filling in the wound, the skin graft needed for the top layer of skin, the epidermis, can be much thinner, allowing for a much quicker healing process.

The scarring in the damaged area is also much less severe, although the new skin that grows over the artificial layer does not look the same (it has no hair, no pigment, and none of the ridges and lines of normal skin).

In 1997 a new, patented artificial skin was approved by the federal Food and Drug Administration (FDA) for use in humans. Due to this invention, thousands of burn patients may not only survive their injuries but may also go on to heal and live better lives without the terrible pain and scarring that previous burn victims have endured.

A Piece of Artificial Skin

The **human immunodeficiency virus**, or **HIV**, could be called modern medicine's Black Plague because of the mystery, prejudice and fear associated with it. Although it has existed at least as far back as the 1950s, because of its long incubation period and gradual spread, it was virtually unknown until the early 1980s.

In 1981, health officials in the U.S. began to notice an increase in certain rare cancers and other diseases. At first, the rise in the death rate seemed to be linked to homosexuals, Haitians and Africans. Then a pattern of occurence was seen among intravenous drug users and patients who had received blood transfusions (see no. 18). Doctors were alarmed by the spread of this syndrome, characterized by the failure of the patients' immune systems. It appeared to be caused by a virus that attacked and destroyed the white blood cells of its victims. Researchers called the new disease acquired immune deficiency syndrome, or AIDS, and began searching for a virus.

The search for the virus was difficult. AIDS affects many parts of the body, with each patient having a unique reaction to the virus. Some patients developed Kaposi's sarcoma, a rare and usually benign cancer (see no. 34). Others fell victim to diseases like tuberculosis (see no. 39) and pneumonia. Still others simply wasted away as their immune systems slowly failed.

Finally, in 1983, a French team of researchers and an American team independently isolated the virus, which was named human immunodeficiency virus. It was found

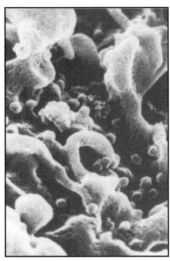

AIDS Virus Magnified

to be spread through the exchange of body fluids. This major discovery proved what many researchers already believed, that the virus was being transmitted by sexual fluids and through the blood. Once the virus and its method of transmission had been identified, it became vitally important to educate the public on how to avoid contracting HIV.

By 1985, methods of checking blood donations had been established to protect recipients of blood transfusions from accidentally receiving the virus from a well-meaning HIV-infected donor. As the death rate continued to rise, health educators focused on spreading information about HIV and its prevention among populations that did not yet show visible signs of infection. Although AIDS had mostly affected male homosexuals, drug abusers, prostitutes and hemophiliacs in the U.S., heterosexually transmitted infection continued to increase and reached epidemic proportions in several African and Asian nations. Unfortunately, while many homosexuals began to practice safe sex, most people in the heterosexual majority incorrectly believed that they were not at risk. It was not until the 1990s that "safe sex," using condoms, and practicing abstinence was understood to be a necessary part of life for everyone.

By 1996, American AIDS researcher **David Ho** (b. 1952) and his colleagues had devised combination drug therapies that were widely successful in reducing the virus to virtually undetectable levels in some patients' bloodstreams. While there was still no cure, for the first time, there was real hope for AIDS victims.

97. Gene Therapy
1990

While the discovery of chromosomes and the structure of DNA were milestones in the study of human genetics and inherited diseases (see nos. 53 and 75), **gene therapy** has become an exciting new development in helping patients that suffer from genetic disorders.

There are three basic forms of gene therapy: gene replacement therapy, in which a normal gene is used to replace a mutant gene; gene augmentation therapy, in which a normal gene is inserted alongside the defective gene into one of the cell's chromosomes; and gene inactivation therapy, in which the normal gene is inserted and neutralizes either a defective protein or an excess number of proteins formed by the abnormal gene. Normal genes can be placed into a cell through either chemical or physical processes. One method uses a **virus**: The normal gene is inserted into the virus, which is then used to "infect" the target cell.

In 1990, U.S. researchers **W. French Anderson**, **Michael Blaese** and **Steven Rosenberg** began the first trials of gene therapy at the National Institute of Health. Their initial experiment involved a child with an immune disorder. The child's white blood cells (see no. 40) could not produce the enzyme adenosine deaminase, or ADA, which is essential for the immune system to develop normally. The doctors used gene augmentation therapy, removing the white blood cells from the child's blood and altering them by adding an ADA gene. These altered cells were then returned to the child's bloodstream. The

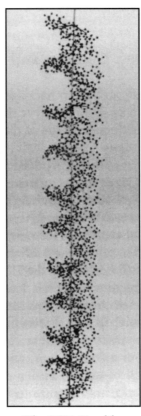

The DNA Double-Helix Molecule

doctors continued this treatment for several months, and early reports indicated that the immune system was working in a more normal manner.

In early 1991 a second gene therapy trial began. It involved two patients suffering from malignant **skin cancer** (see no. 34). In this trial, a different method of gene transfer was used. Researchers set up the body's own defenses to attack the cancer by encasing copies of the genes for a protein called HLA-B7 into droplets of fat. This allowed the DNA to pass into the cancer cells when the fat was injected directly into the tumors. Then, when the gene-activated cancer cells began producing HLA-B7, the body's white blood cells were attracted to the tumor, destroying the malignant cells. Other trials to treat genetic diseases such as cystic fibrosis, hemophilia and muscular dystrophy are in the process of being developed.

While these trials are encouraging, gene therapy must undergo much more research and more trials before it will be an accepted treatment. In addition, with the increased ability to diagnose and predict genetic disorders, there is concern that the patient's privacy may be invaded. For example, if testing showed that the patient had inherited genes that were likely to cause a long disease resulting in death, the patient might be denied medical benefits due to this "pre-existing condition." Hopefully, the possibility of effective treatment with gene therapy will avoid this sort of discrimination.

98. Fetal Surgery
1994

As medicine has progressed, surgeons have attempted greater feats of surgery in the effort to save lives. One of the most tragic events in a surgeon's career is watching a newborn baby die because of its birth defects.

Once, blue babies always died because of the heart defect they were born with. However, with the advent of open heart surgery (see no. 71), these babies are now often saved and live long and productive lives. Another tragic birth defect is the diaphragmatic hernia. In this case, there is a hole in the baby's diaphragm, the muscle that divides the chest from the abdomen. As the baby develops in the womb, parts of the stomach, spleen, intestines or liver move up into the chest cavity, preventing the lungs from developing. When the baby is born, it dies, unable to breathe.

When American medical intern **Michael Harrison** (b. 1943) witnessed a newborn baby with a diaphragmatic hernia die, he wondered if there was a way to save these babies. If doctors couldn't repair the damage after birth, was there a way to repair it before birth? Nine years later, he gathered a research team at the University of California San Francisco Medical Center. They began experimenting on unborn sheep with diaphragmatic hernias. They found that once they had moved the organs back into the abdomen, the lungs grew rapidly and the lambs survived.

By 1994, Harrison and his team had already attempted surgery several times. Finally, they were successful. It was tiny **Maggie Macala Denis** who survived the delicate surgery. First Harrison opened the mother's womb, exposing the baby's chest and abdomen. He removed her partially from the womb, and operated, putting her intestines and spleen back into her abdomen and repairing her diaphragm. Then he placed her back into the womb. Maggie was born seven weeks later at three pounds, 11 ounces by Cesarean section — an operation to remove a baby from the womb when birth does not progress normally.

More recently, **fetal surgery** has been used to save babies from other fatal defects, including such problems as blocked urinary tracts, which can destroy the babies' bladder and kidneys. Along with the new experimental methods of growing tissue and new organs (see no. 100), Harrison's surgical techniques are opening up a new frontier in medicine.

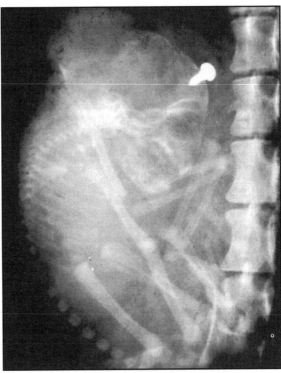

Fetal Monkey With Shunt in the Brain

Cloning
1997

A clone is a genetically identical organism created directly from one cell of another individual. **Cloning** occurs naturally when a living cell divides, as with single-celled organisms like the amoeba. In human reproduction, natural cloning results in identical twins when the fertilized egg splits, producing two identical beings. The egg can split more than once, providing identical triplets, quadruplets or even quintuplets.

Frogs have been cloned from the cell of an existing animal in the laboratory, but it was the successful in vitro fertilization of human eggs (see no. 94) that led to the "cloning" of humans in 1993. By dividing a fertilized human egg at a very early stage of development in the petri dish, an identical twin was produced. This technique had already been successful with sheep and other animals.

In human experiments, cells from aborted embryos were used for early cloning attempts and later discarded. This practice provoked an outcry from religious people who felt that using embryos in such procedures should be banned.

Then in 1997, the entire world was stunned by the announcement that Scottish researcher **Ian Wilmut** (b. 1945) had successfully cloned a sheep. Working at the Roslin Institute in Edinburgh, Scotland, Wilmut's team took the egg of one variety of sheep, inserted the genetic material from another adult sheep into the egg, and reinserted the egg into the womb of the first sheep. When "Dolly" was born, she was obviously of the same variety as the adult sheep that the genetic material had been taken from — not the variety of sheep from which the egg cell had been taken. DNA testing proved that the experiment had been a complete success —Dolly was an exact clone of the other sheep — and that she was developing normally.

While the ethical controversy raged over Wilmut's experiments, only a few months later, the Oregon Regional Primate Research Center announced that they had cloned rhesus monkeys by a similar process, using cells from embryos rather than from adult monkeys. According to **Donald Wolf** (b. 1939), one of the center's senior scientists, this cloning procedure can produce genetically identical monkeys that will simplify medical research. One result of this technique would be that fewer animals will need to be used in research because of the uniformity of the clones.

Due to ethical and religious concerns, **President Bill Clinton** asked that federal money not be spent on cloning humans. In early 1998, physician **Richard Seeds** announced that he would clone a human baby. Public opposition was immediate, and President Clinton and the U.S. Congress acted quickly to make human cloning illegal in the U.S.

Identical Twins

While new methods for the transplantation of human skin, tissues and organs have improved the quality of life and extended the lives of many patients, the most innovative technique in transplantation was announced on July 23, 1997, by British doctors **Anthony Atala** and **Dario Fauza** at a conference of the British Association of Pediatric Surgeons. Atala and Fauza's new technique of growing organs has been used to literally build bladders and windpipes for sheep, leg muscles for a rabbit, and a kidney for a rat. Using the animal's own cells and using molds to help the tissues take shape, the doctors have found a way to avoid the problem of rejection of donor organs (see no. 74). Since the tissue is grown from the patient's own cells, the body accepts it as normal tissue, avoiding the need for anti-rejection drugs, which have many undesirable side effects (see no. 89).

Atala and Fauza believed that their technique for growing new organs could be used to correct many common birth defects. With this use in mind, they formulated a method for growing replacement organs for babies while they are still in the womb. For example, if doctors detected a defect in the baby's bladder, they would operate on the baby six months into the pregnancy. Using tiny incisions, they would insert a surgical camera and use an endoscope (see no. 86) to remove a pea-sized sample of the bladder. Lab technicians would separate the different types of cells, placing them into a clear solution that is rich in proteins and nutrients. Then the dishes of solution would be placed into an incubator.

Body tissues grow at an amazing pace in the ideal conditions of an incubator. One square centimeter of tissue can grow to cover two football fields within two months. This fact could allow the doctors to build a new organ before the infant was born. They could build an organ by placing the new tissues over

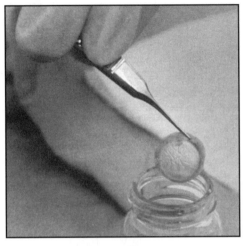

Human Cornea

biodegradable forms. Within six weeks of the first surgery, the new bladder would be ready for transplantation into the newborn. Only minutes after birth, the transplant would be performed, and the baby would have a new and fully functional bladder.

This amazing innovation has given doctors and patients hope that new hearts, kidneys, bladders and other organs will soon be grown in the laboratory. This might save thousands of lives every year, since transplant patients will no longer have to wait for a suitable organ donor, and then endure the possibility of rejection and taking anti-rejection medications for the rest of their lives. Doctors will not have to place patients on waiting lists, knowing that as their health declines, they will be moved closer to the top of the list, but also that they might become too ill or weak for the surgery if a donor organ becomes available.

Tests on humans to perform transplants of laboratory-grown replacement organs were scheduled to begin in 1998, and Atala and Fauza hoped to have approval from the Food and Drug Administration (FDA) for routine use of the technique within five years.

TRIVIA QUIZ & PROJECT SUGGESTIONS

1. What were the "miracle cures" and "wonder drugs" of the 20th century? Tell the strange story of how one was discovered by accident. (see nos. 64, 70, 72, 77 and 85)

2. What happened to the boy who was bitten by the rabid dog? Who or what saved him? (see no. 38)

3. What epidemic seemed like it could be the Black Death of the 20th century? (see no. 96)

4. Whose work was followed for centuries before someone discovered that he was wrong? (see no. 5) Who found the mistakes and corrected them? (see no. 6 and no. 8)

5. What practice did the Yellow Emperor advocate, and when was it "discovered" by modern medicine? (see no. 4)

6. Who discovered how the stomach works? How was he able to see it happen? (see no. 26)

7. What famous aviator helped build the very first artificial heart? (see no. 92)

8. How do doctors help burn victims? What is the greatest danger to the patient? (see no. 95)

9. Who used limes to cure a common disease among sailors? What was the disease? What did Captain Cook have to do with it? (see no. 12)

10. When did doctors learn that they have to wash their hands? Why? (see no. 22)

11. Why didancient doctors drill holes in their patients' heads? What do modern doctors do instead? (see no. 37)

12. What was the Guinea Pig Club? Why did they call themselves that? (see no. 68)

13. What is Hansen's disease? Why was it so terrifying to people? Is there a cure? (see no. 35)

14. What did rats carry into the cities in the Middle Ages? When was an effective treatment discovered? (see no. 41)

15. Who found a way to help patients with emotional disturbances? What did they name this new branch of science? What doctor discovered that some mental problems are caused by chemical imbalances? (see nos. 42 and 73)

16. What is the process of creating an identical organism called? Why are people so upset about this process? (see no. 99)

17. Who was the first "test-tube" baby? Why did the doctors develop this technique? (see no. 94)

18. What diseases do mosquitoes carry? Who discovered this, and what did they do to stop the mosquitoes? (see nos. 45and 46)

19. When did doctors discover ways to prevent a disease before it starts? Describe some ways this can be done. (see no. 81)

20. What was the first clinical precision instrument used for medical diagnosis? (see no. 11)

21. Who found tiny creatures in pond water? How could he see them? What else did he discover? (see no. 9)

SUGGESTED PROJECTS

1a. How has the discovery of immunizations changed your world? Interview your parents and grandparents about all of the diseases that used to be common in child hood. For example, did they have the measles? Smallpox? Polio? Did anyone that they knew have any of these diseases? How did it affect them as they grew up? If they had a friend or family member that had polio, what precautions did their parents take to try to avoid spreading the disease? Do they remember the day that the polio vaccine became available? What did the parents in their town or city do to celebrate? Are there any other serious diseases or hereditary conditions in your family history?

1b. After you have interviewed your family, go to the library and look up old newspaper articles about these diseases. The librarian can help you find all the information that you need. Look up the years that your parents and grandparents were sick. Make copies of the articles about these diseases and how they affected your town. Then take your interviews and the newspaper articles and make a family medical history book.

2. Epidemic diseases changed the entire cultures of England and Europe. Research how and why the Black Death led to democracy. Which countries were most affected and which were affected the least? Were countries like Norway more or less affected by the Black Death? Why? Were there other influences which determined these differences, such as climate or social customs? Were crowded cities more affected than the countrysides? Explain how these different conditions may have affected the spread of the disease.

3. Penicillin was isolated from a mold culture. Grow some mold in jars: In each jar, put a different food, such as cheese, bread, apple slices, and so on. Sprinkle some water into each jar and put a lid on it. In a few days, you should have a variety of mold cultures. Then take samples from each jar and look at them under a micro scope. How are the molds different? How are the same? Can you think of any other important medicines or foods that were developed from molds?

4. AIDS is a terrible disease. What other diseases have affected humankind for centuries, but have finally been cured? How were they cured? Did researchers find medicines or vaccines? Are there any diseases that no longer exist because of modern medicine? Write a short paper on this subject.

5. Do you know how to use the Internet to look for information about diseases? There are several Web sites where you can look up information about famous doctors and scientists as well as diseases and their treatments. Look for health information on AOL at http://www.aol.com/netfind/time savers/health.html and in the U.S. National Library of Medicine at http://www.nlm. nih.gov/. There are also many interesting sites like Louisiana State University Libraries, which indexes the scientists profiled in The Faces of Science: African Americans in the Sciences. The Internet address is http://www.lib.lsu.edu/lib/chem/ display/alphabetic.html. There are many other places on the Internet where you can search for specific information. If you are not on the Internet, you can go to your local library. Many now have com puters where you can look up information and access the Internet.

INDEX

INDEX

INDEX